D1236752

WHERE HAVE ALL THE BEES GONE?

Pollinators in Crisis

Where Have All The

BE

ES

Gone?

REBECCA E. HIRSCH

TWENTY-FIRST CENTURY BOOKS / MINNEAPOLIS

To the bees, with thanks for all you do —R.H.

Twenty-First Century Books
An imprint of Lerner Publishing Group, Inc.
241 First Avenue North
Minneapolis, MN 55401 USA

For reading levels and more information,
look up this title at www.lernerbooks.com.

Main body text set in ITC Caslon 224 Std Book.
Typeface provided by Adobe Systems.

Library of Congress Cataloging-in-Publication Data

Names: Hirsch, Rebecca E., author.
Title: Where have all the bees gone? : pollinators in crisis / by Rebecca E.
    Hirsch.
Description: Minneapolis : Twenty-First Century Books, [2020] | Audience:
    Age 13–18. | Audience: Grade 9 to 12. | Includes bibliographical
    references and index. |
Identifiers: LCCN 2019020684 (print) | LCCN 2019021603 (ebook) | ISBN
    9781541583856 (eb pdf) | ISBN 9781541534636 (lb : alk. paper)
Subjects: LCSH: Bees—Conservation—Juvenile literature. | Insect
    pollinators—Conservation—Juvenile literature. | Pollination by bees—
    Juvenile literature.
Classification: LCC QL568.A6 (ebook) | LCC QL568.A6 H485 2020 (print) |
    DDC 595.79/9—dc23

LC record available at https://lccn.loc.gov/2019020684

Manufactured in the United States of America
1-44880-35729-8/7/2019

Contents

1
The Last Franklin's Bumblebee   6

2
An Ancient Relationship   14

3
Pollination Powerhouses   24

4
A Bee Cs   34

5
Disease Spillover   48

6
The Day the Bees Died   62

7
Bee Town, USA   72

8
What's Best for Bees?   82

A Note from the Author   92
Glossary   93
Source Notes   95
Selected Bibliography   99
Further Information   100
Index   102

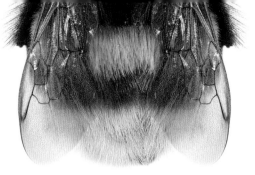

1

The Last Franklin's Bumblebee

People often ask the value of Franklin's bumblebee. In terms of a direct contribution to the grand scale of human economies, perhaps not much, but no one has measured its contribution in those terms. However, in the grand scheme of our planet and its environmental values, I would say it is priceless.

—Robbin Thorp, entomologist

Robbin Thorp, wearing a bright yellow T-shirt with a bumblebee printed across the front, drives his white truck along a road on Mount Ashland in southern Oregon. He steers past the base of a ski lift and rolls to a stop beside an alpine meadow. He cuts the engine and steps out into the sunshine.

Under a sky of blue streaked white with clouds, the meadow blazes with pink and yellow flowers. But Thorp focuses on something other than the fine weather and quiet scenery. He is on a quest.

Thorp is a retired entomologist (a scientist who studies insects). He is searching for the bee pictured on his shirt: Franklin's bumblebee. It looks much like any other of North America's forty-six species of bumblebee—big, fat, and fuzzy. Unlike other

A bee flies through a meadow, looking for the nectar it needs to survive.

bumblebees, it has a round, black face and a U-shaped marking on its back, right between the wings.

As far as bumblebees go, Franklin's isn't remarkable, except for one thing: it has gone missing. Once common in alpine meadows like this one, the bee seems to have vanished. Thorp hasn't seen one in ten years.

Slowly, Thorp walks from flower to flower, shoes crunching on the craggy ground. In one hand, he holds a white net and in the other, a device like a squirt gun. But this device doesn't shoot water. It slurps bees.

As he walks, he peers at each clump of flowers and inspects the bees that are busily looking for food there. When he sees a bee that deserves a closer look, he pauses, leans forward, raises the bee vacuum, and takes aim.

ZEEEEEOOOP!

He studies the imprisoned creature through a magnifying lens built into the vacuum. He looks for the telltale markings. Is it "that bee"—the one on his shirt? The one he seeks? Is it a Franklin's?

Again and again, with each bee he finds, the answer is no. What has happened to Franklin's bumblebee?

DISAPPEARING BEES

The story of the disappearance of Franklin's bumblebee begins in the 1990s. That's when US Forest Service officials approached Thorp, who was then a professor at the University of California–Davis, and asked him to monitor the species. At the time, *Bombus franklini* (the bee's scientific name) had the smallest geographic range of any of the world's 250 species of bumblebees. The rare bee lived only in southern Oregon and Northern California, between the Cascade Range and the Pacific Ocean. Its entire range could fit inside an oval just 200 miles (322 km) north to south and 70 miles (113 km) east to west.

Because the chubby bee with the round black face and the *U* on its back was so rare, Forest Service officials wondered whether it should be listed as endangered. An endangered species is one at risk of going extinct, or completely disappearing from Earth.

The US Endangered Species Act of 1973 protects animals and plants in the United States that are in danger of becoming extinct. When the US government adds a species to the endangered species list, federal agencies must conserve and protect the species and its habitat—the environment in which the plant or animal normally lives. Agencies must prohibit actions that would harm the species, such as hunting it or destroying forests. The act has saved several animals from extinction. The bald eagle, peregrine falcon, brown pelican, and American alligator all came dangerously close to extinction but rebounded with protection from the Endangered

WHAT'S IN A NAME?

All plants and animals have common names, such as the Shasta daisy and the peregrine falcon. Biologists also use a scientific naming system created by Swedish scientist Carolus Linnaeus in the mid-eighteenth century. The system uses Latin-based terms to identify each plant or animal's genus (group) and species (specific kind within that group). For example, all bumblebees belong to the same genus, *Bombus*, so all share that first name. Each species within *Bombus* has a distinct second name. Franklin's bumblebee is called *Bombus franklini*, while the western bumblebee is *Bombus occidentalis*.

Genus and species are the most precise classifications for living things. But these categories fall under a larger naming umbrella of eight levels: domain, kingdom, phylum, class, order, family, genus, and species. You can see the hierarchy by looking at Franklin's bumblebee. It belongs to the domain Eukarya, a group that includes all plants and animals. Within that category, Franklin's bumblebee belongs to the kingdom Animalia (the animal kingdom), the phylum Arthropoda (animals with jointed legs and no backbones), the class Insecta (insects), the order Hymenoptera (a group of insects including ants, wasps, and bees), the family Apidae (bees), and the genus *Bombus* (bumblebees). The species name *Bombus franklini* is the designation for Franklin's bumblebee. Each kind of living thing has its own species name, and members of the same species can mate with one another.

Species Act. Was Franklin's bumblebee a good candidate for protection?

Thorp agreed to help find answers. He began driving several times a year into the heart of Franklin's territory and counting bumblebees. Within this small region, the bee was common. "I could walk down and see [Franklin's bumblebees] on every patch of flowers," he recalled.

That first year was 1998. He counted ninety-four Franklin's bumblebees, which seemed like a normal number to him. The next year, he found only twenty, but he didn't think much of it. Bee populations fluctuate. Then the population dropped off a cliff. "All of a sudden," he said, "the bees disappeared out from under me."

In 2000 he found only nine, and in 2001, just one. The number of sightings climbed to twenty in 2002 but dropped to just three the next year. He didn't see the bee at all in 2004 or 2005.

Then came 2006. "August ninth," he said. "I've got that [date] indelibly emblazoned in my mind."

He was combing the meadow on Oregon's Mount Ashland, the one past the ski lift, when he saw a bee on a flower. He recognized it instantly as a Franklin's. The bee flew off, and Thorp ran after it down the hill, his heart pounding. He never caught the bee. Throughout the day and in the years that followed, he returned to the site repeatedly, but he never saw another sign of the species.

What had caused this bee to go *poof*? And could it be happening to other bees?

MORE BEES GO MISSING

Around the time Robbin Thorp watched the decline of Franklin's bumblebee, biologist John Ascher was looking for bumblebees in California. He couldn't find the western bumblebee (*Bombus occidentalis*), a close relative of Franklin's. That was odd, because the western bumblebee was supposed to be one of the most common bumblebees in the region stretching from California northward to Alaska.

Ascher moved to Ithaca, New York, to earn a PhD in entomology at Cornell University. At first, he found three eastern bumblebee species in upstate New York: the rusty patched bumblebee (*Bombus*

Researchers John Ascher (*left*) and Kevin Matteson collect bees from a flowering cherry tree in Central Park in New York City. Ascher identified several declining bee species in New York State.

THE RUSTY PATCHED BUMBLEBEE

The rusty patched bumblebee appears to be at serious risk of extinction. Despite intensive and repeated searches, it has not been found in most of its range since 2003. The bee was listed as endangered under the Species at Risk Act in Canada in 2010.

After years of pressure by scientists, conservation groups, and concerned citizens, in 2017 the US government agreed to list the bee under the US Endangered Species Act. The listing was a huge victory for bumblebee conservation because federal agencies must take steps to protect the bee's remaining habitat and help conserve the species.

To protect the few remaining rusty patched bumblebees, the United States added the species to the endangered list in 2017.

affinis), the yellow-banded bumblebee (*Bombus terricola*), and Ashton's bumblebee (*Bombus ashtoni*). But in 2001, all three species began to disappear. "It would be like if you went out one day and there were no cardinals, or there were no mockingbirds anymore," Ascher said. "It's that obvious to bee people."

He wasn't the only one to notice. Between 2004 and 2006, biologists Sheila Colla and Laurence Packer at York University in Toronto carried out field surveys, counting bumblebees in the southern part of Ontario, a province in Canada. They compared their results to counts of Ontario's bumblebees from the 1970s. Colla and Packer could find only eleven species, down from fourteen that had lived in the area in the 1970s. Of the eleven remaining bee species, four were much rarer than they had been in the previous study. To Colla and Packer, those four species appeared to be in decline.

Even more troubling, Colla and Packer searched extensively for one of the missing species, a bee with an orange patch on its back known as the rusty patched bumblebee. Before the 1990s, it could be found throughout central and eastern North America. Colla and Packer looked and looked. They traveled to eighteen sites in eastern Canada and thirty-five sites across fourteen US states. All were places where the bee had lived. Mostly, the researchers came up empty. They found only one rusty patched bumblebee foraging (gathering food) on a sunflower in a park in Ontario. They found none in the United States.

Bumblebee disappearances, first reported by Thorp and soon by others, sent alarm bells through the world of bee scientists. What was happening to North America's bumblebees?

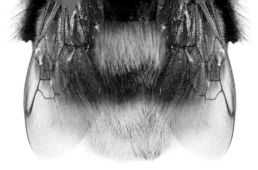
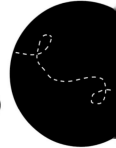

2

An Ancient Relationship

It took hundreds of millions of years to produce the life that now inhabits the earth—eons of time in which that developing and evolving and diversifying life reached a state of adjustment and balance with its surroundings. . . . Given time—time not in years but in millennia—life adjusts, and a balance has been reached. For time is the essential ingredient; but in the modern world there is no time.

—Rachel Carson, biologist and naturalist

Once, 140 million years ago, no bees lived on Earth. If you could travel back to that time, you would be at the end of the age of the dinosaurs, a time known as the Cretaceous period. Dinosaurs great and small roamed forests of ferns, conifers (cone-bearing trees), and cycads (palmlike trees that also have cones). Herds of iguanodons grazed on horsetails, and meat-eating neovenators prowled among the herds. In the skies overhead, small feathered dinosaurs—the first birds—soared alongside pterosaurs with giant, 40-foot (12 m) wingspans. Mammals lived in this world too. Small and furry, they hid in the shadows and came out at night. If you looked closely, you might see wasps hunting among the foliage for insect prey. If you listened, you might hear the whine of mosquitoes and the whir of

At the beginning of the Cretaceous period, when dinosaurs roamed, the world had no flowering plants and no bees to pollinate them.

giant dragonflies. But you would hear no murmuring hum of bees, for this was the world as it appeared before bees.

Then something new arrived, something revolutionary from a biological point of view. That something was a flower, and it would open the way for bees.

 ## THE SEX LIVES OF PLANTS

Plants have sex—they carry out sexual reproduction with other plants of the same species. This sex has always presented a problem for plants. Plants are rooted in the ground, so they can't move from place to place. Since they can't move, they can't carry their pollen—grains that carry sperm, or male sex cells—to the eggs, or female sex cells, of another plant. Since plants can't move their pollen themselves, they require a courier, or carrier.

ASSISTED REPRODUCTION

Flowers attract bees (and other insects, such as butterflies, flies, and beetles) with their scents, shapes, and colors. As a bee forages for pollen and nectar on a flower, it brushes against the flower's anthers. These male reproductive organs are full of pollen. Some of the pollen grains stick to the feathery hairs on the bee's body. As the bee continues to visit other flowers of the same species, it might unknowingly transfer some of this pollen from its body to the new flower's stigma, the female reproductive organ.

After a pollen grain lands on a stigma, it delivers two sperm cells to an ovule, or egg cell, at the base of the flower. One of the sperm cells fertilizes the egg cell, producing a single seed. The other sperm cell develops into a nutrient-rich tissue that surrounds the seed—the fruit.

As the fruit ripens, it changes. The fruit of apricots, plums, cherries, and berries becomes soft and sweet. This fruit lures hungry animals, which eat the fruit. The seeds pass through their bodies and return to the ground in their dung. Other fruits become dry and lightweight—perfect for wind travel. Examples are the winged maple seed or a dandelion seed with its tiny parachute. The fruit of the coconut tree becomes hard and watertight. It might fall into a body of water and float away from the parent plant. Whether carried away by animals, wind, or water, the seed inside the fruit waits for its basic needs to be met. Those needs are water, an ideal temperature (which varies from species to species), and loose soil with plenty of oxygen. When these conditions are met, the seed cracks open. A root pushes downward into the soil. A shoot stretches upward toward the light. And a new plant begins.

POLLINATION BETWEEN FLOWERING PLANTS OF THE SAME SPECIES

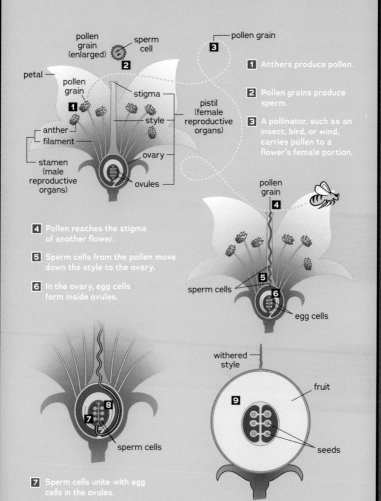

pollen grain (enlarged)

sperm cell

2

petal

pollen grain

1

anther

filament

stamen (male reproductive organs)

stigma

style

pistil (female reproductive organs)

ovary

ovules

pollen grain

3

1 Anthers produce pollen.

2 Pollen grains produce sperm.

3 A pollinator, such as an insect, bird, or wind, carries pollen to a flower's female portion.

pollen grain

4

sperm cells

5

6

egg cells

4 Pollen reaches the stigma of another flower.

5 Sperm cells from the pollen move down the style to the ovary.

6 In the ovary, egg cells form inside ovules.

8

7

sperm cells

withered style

fruit

9

seeds

7 Sperm cells unite with egg cells in the ovules.

8 The ovules become seeds.

9 The ovary develops into a fruit with seeds.

An Ancient Relationship

An early solution, a method used for millions of years by conifers and cycads (and still used in the twenty-first century), was to toss pollen into the wind. The male cones of these trees produce clouds of pollen, and the wind carries it to female cones, where eggs reside. Wind pollination works, but it is wasteful and inefficient, with low rates of fertilization. Conifers must make huge amounts of pollen, most of which never reach a female cone.

But flowering plants, called angiosperms, developed a better way of spreading pollen. The first angiosperms, somewhere between 190 and 150 million years ago, began to house all their sex organs, both male and female, in a cluster surrounded by petals—a flower. Pollen is rich in protein, an important nutrient, so some winged insects began to eat it. As ancient insects visited the first flowers, searching for pollen to eat, some of the pollen stuck to their bodies. As the insects moved from flower to flower, they unknowingly moved the pollen on their bodies from the male parts of flowers to the female parts of flowers, helping plants reproduce. These insect go-betweens were much more effective at moving pollen than wind. And because they were so effective, the odds for fertilization improved and more plants were able to reproduce.

THE BIRTH OF BEES

In the early days of flowering plants, beetles and flies were the primary pollinators. Then a group of meat-eating wasps made the switch to a diet of pollen. They evolved into Earth's first bees. That ancient switch, which happened about 130 million years ago, launched bees down a unique path.

The first flowers on Earth were dull in color—pale white or green—and the petals were wide open, with pollen in easy reach. Early flowering plants evolved, or changed from one generation to the next. Scientists think they evolved with the help of insects. Here's how: Plants and animals of the same species are all a little different.

DARWIN'S "ABOMINABLE MYSTERY"

In travels around the world and in laboratory studies, British naturalist Charles Darwin (1809–1882) observed nature in all its forms. He concluded that the great diversity of life on Earth arose slowly over millions of years. In his 1859 book *On the Origin of Species*, he gave his explanation of how this works—the theory of evolution by natural selection. According to this theory, living things that have traits to help them survive and produce more offspring—such as bright, showy flowers—pass these traits to the next generation. So certain traits become more common and others die out. Sometimes the changes are so great that new species develop. According to Darwin, this slowly but steadily led to the vast diversity of species.

Naturalist Charles Darwin believed that flowering plants evolved quickly on Earth because of the bees and other insects that helped them reproduce.

Yet flowering plants vexed Darwin. Twenty years after publishing his theory of evolution, he described their evolution as an "abominable mystery." His research showed that a huge variety of flowering plants seem to have popped up suddenly in the Cretaceous period. They hadn't evolved slowly and gradually but had appeared in quick bursts. How had flowering plants evolved so quickly?

Darwin later came to believe, as do some modern biologists, that a driving force behind the rapid rise of flowering plants was their interaction with insect pollinators, especially bees. This interaction may have been a big reason why flowering plants evolved so quickly and spread so widely. Plants pollinated by insects produced more seeds and more offspring, which gave them a leg up over plants that were not pollinated by insects. Plants and insects evolved together, and this coevolution led to the spectacular rise of both groups.

An Ancient Relationship

That was true of species of early flowering plants. Some flowers were a little bigger, or smaller, than those of other plants of the same species. Some were duller in color or a little more brightly colored. Some were more fragrant. A bigger, brighter flower likely stood out in the mostly green Cretaceous landscape, with all the ferns, conifers, and cycads. Bigger, brighter flowers attracted more insect pollinators.

ANCIENT EVIDENCE

How do scientists know when the first bees appeared on Earth? They have pieced together clues about the past from two types of evidence. First, they look at ancient bees trapped in amber, or hardened tree sap. Such bees are extremely rare. In 2006 George Poinar Jr., an entomology professor at Oregon State University, found an ancient bee in an amber mine in the South Asian nation of Myanmar. Based on the age of the rocks surrounding the mine, Poinar determined that the bee was one hundred million years old. It was the oldest bee ever discovered.

Other scientists have pushed the date of the first bee back even further by looking at a different type of evidence: deoxyribonucleic acid, or DNA, the genetic material found in bees, wasps, and all living things. As living things evolve from generation to generation, their DNA mutates, or changes, slowly over time. In this way, wasps evolved to become bees, and early plants evolved to become flowering plants, for example. If the two groups split very recently, their DNA will be very much alike—because DNA changes slowly over generations. But if the split was more ancient, their DNA will have more differences, because more and more changes will pile up over the generations. Studies that compare the DNA of wasps and bees reveal that bees appeared perhaps 130 million years ago or even earlier. This places the first bee soon after plants evolved the first flowers.

So did more fragrant flowers. With higher rates of pollination, plants with attractive flowers produced more offspring than plants with lower rates of pollination. The plants with appealing flowers passed their traits down to the next generation, which also had big, bright, and fragrant flowers. Generation by generation, flowers of certain species became bigger, brighter, showier, and more fragrant. They continued to attract more pollinators and to reproduce successfully across generations. Meanwhile, plants with dull-colored flowers were less likely to reproduce, and some of them died out.

As flowers evolved and changed, insects evolved and changed too. The first bees closely resembled their wasp ancestors. They had short tongues and sleek, mostly hairless bodies. Over time, early bees became hairy, because more pollen sticks to a hairy body than to a hairless one. Some bees, such as honeybees and bumblebees, developed corbiculae, baskets on their legs for carrying pollen. Others developed scopae, stiff pollen-collecting hairs, on their thoraxes (upper bodies) or abdomens. Some evolved longer tongues to reach nectar deep inside flowers.

Together, they transformed the landscape. At the start of the Cretaceous period, ferns, conifers, and cycads dominated the land. There were no angiosperms. And because flowering plants develop berries and fruits, which hold their seeds, there were no berries or fruits either. But by the close of the period, flowering plants outnumbered the ferns, conifers, and cycads, and forests resembled those found in many parts of North America in modern times, full of oaks, hickories, and magnolias.

END OF AN ERA

The Cretaceous closed with a bang. Sixty-five million years ago, an asteroid roughly 6 miles (10 km) across smashed into Earth, hitting at roughly the site of the Yucatán Peninsula of eastern Mexico. The impact threw dust and debris into the air, churned up huge tidal

As they buzz around flowers looking for nectar, bees get covered in pollen. Some of this pollen ends up on the flowers' female reproductive organs, leading to fertilization.

waves, and set off volcanic eruptions. The volcanoes spewed more dust into the air. All the dust blocked sunlight, reducing the heat and light that reached the surface of the planet. Many plants and animals were unable to adapt to this new, cooler environment. Perhaps half the world's species went extinct.

Nearly all large animals, including most of the dinosaurs, died out. Only one line, the birds, survived. Many smaller life-forms made it through, including our own ancestors, the furry and warm-blooded mammals. All major lines of insects survived, including bees. So did most of the flowering plants.

Life on Earth bounced back. In the twenty-first century, flowering plants continue to dominate ecosystems. Nearly 90 percent of all existing land plants are angiosperms—somewhere around 250,000 to 300,000 species. They flourish in every type of environment around the world—from lush forests and vast grasslands to scorching deserts and frozen tundra. And wherever you find flowering plants, you'll find their main pollinators—the twenty thousand or so species of bees.

3

Pollination Powerhouses

We must save the bees to save ourselves.

—Sheila Colla, biologist

More than twenty thousand species of bees live around the world. That's more than all the reptiles, amphibians, birds, and mammals on Earth *combined*.

Bees live on every continent except Antarctica and in nearly every type of environment: in forests, on mountains, and in meadows. You'll find bees anywhere there are flowering plants. Their relationship with flowers makes bees so important.

Flowering plants include the ones we think of as flowers: orchids and daisies, roses and magnolias. They also include fruits, from peaches and plums to apples and apricots. They include foods we think of as vegetables: carrots, cabbages, beans, bell peppers, onions, tomatoes, and garlic. They include almonds, walnuts,

A bee gathers nectar from a sunflower and picks up a coating of pollen.

cashews, peanuts, pistachios—every kind of nut except pine nuts (which come from pine cones). They include maple, birch, willow, and oak trees. Flowering plants make up most of the botanical world. They greatly outnumber the nonflowering plants: the mosses, ferns, and conifers. Bees are so important because they pollinate so many of the plants we rely on for food, wood, and other products.

Bees aren't the only animals that transfer pollen between the male and female parts of flowering plants. More than two hundred thousand animal species, including birds, bats, butterflies, moths, and beetles, help pollinate the world's flowering plants. But bees transfer more pollen than any other type of animal. "There's no question that bees are the most important in most ecosystems," says Rachael Winfree, an ecologist at Rutgers University in New Jersey. She calls bees "the 800-pound [365 kg] gorillas" (most dominant force) of the pollinator world.

WORLD OF POLLINATORS

All sorts of creatures pollinate flowers. Swarms of flies are attracted to flowers that smell like rotten meat. These putrid blooms fool the flies, who think they have found rotting flesh on which to lay their eggs. While they are looking for a place to lay eggs, the flies end up pollinating the plant. In desert and tropical climates, bats pollinate many flowers. The bats have long tongues that they use to drink nectar from large, bowl-shaped blossoms. Beetles are clumsy fliers and prefer wide, open flowers or flower clusters that give them an easy place to land. Hummingbirds, the smallest birds in the world, can hover in midair as they dine, beating their wings up to eighty times per second as they lap nectar with their long, forked tongues.

On the island of Madagascar in the Indian Ocean, black-and-white ruffed lemurs pollinate traveler's trees. This primate is about the size of a house cat. The lemurs climb high into traveler's trees and use their nimble hands to pry open the tough leaves that surround the large flowers. Then the lemurs stick in their snouts, drink nectar, and come out with pollen all over their faces. The lemurs travel from tree to tree, drinking nectar, and pollinating the plants. These lemurs are the largest pollinators on Earth.

Bees aren't the only pollinators on the planet. As it searches for nectar, the black-and-white ruffed lemur pollinates a species of tree on the island of Madagascar.

GOOD VIBRATIONS

What makes bees such outstanding pollinators? Efficiency. Bees run the most efficient pollen-delivery service of any member of the insect world. Bees raise their young on pollen. So the number of offspring they leave behind, what biologists call their reproductive success, is tied to the number of flowers they visit. With reproductive success on the line, bees have evolved to be highly motivated to visit as many flowers in a day as they can. Being hairy also helps. The hairy bodies of bees are spectacularly evolved to mop up pollen. If you inspect the hair of a bee under a microscope, you will see that it is feathered—each hair shaft has many small branches. Feathering increases the surface area of each hair, which allows it to hold more pollen.

Bees also get a boost from electricity. As a bee flies, its tiny hairs bump into electrically charged particles in the air. The bee's body acquires a positive electrical charge from those particles. Flowers tend to be negatively charged, and negative and positive charges attract each other. As a positively charged bee approaches a negatively charged flower, the pollen literally flies from the flower to the bee, drawn by static electricity. This process is similar to when you rub your stocking feet on the carpet and then get a zap when you touch a doorknob. With a similar zap, pollen hops onto the bee's body, even before the bee has landed on a flower.

On most flowers, pollen is easily accessible to bees and other insects. An insect merely has to brush against the anther of a flower to get a dusting of pollen. But a few flowers, including blueberries, cranberries, tomatoes, eggplants, and peppers, keep their pollen locked inside narrow tube-shaped anthers. Only bumblebees and a few other wild bees can reach this pollen. They use buzz pollination, or sonication. The bee wraps its legs around the pollen-filled anther and vibrates its body. This rapid movement creates a high-pitched buzzing sound. The vibration of the buzzing rattles the pollen from the anthers. The pollen pours out, like salt from a shaker. According to Denise Ellsworth, an entomologist at Ohio State University, the high-pitched sound is the musical note of middle C. "It's the [same note as] 'hey' in [the Beatles' song] 'Hey Jude,'" said Ellsworth, "and it causes the flower to explosively release pollen."

Bees vary greatly in the flowers they prefer. Bumblebees and honeybees are generalists, visiting a wide range of flowers. But many solitary bees are finicky. Which flowers a bee visits depends on the shape and size of its body and, importantly, on the length of its tongue. Bees with short tongues pollinate flowers that are wide open, with nectar in easy reach, like goldenrod. Bees with long tongues can access nectar hidden in deep flowers, like columbine. Much also depends on timing, which flowers are in bloom at the time of day or the season when a particular bee is active and flying around.

BEES = FOOD

Without bees, we wouldn't have food. On farms, bees pollinate apples, berries, melons, pumpkins, almonds, and cherries. They pollinate peppers, cucumbers, eggplants, tomatoes—even cotton and coffee. Wind pollinates the grains, such as corn, wheat, and rye, but bees pollinate almost everything else. They pollinate 75 percent of the fruits, vegetables, and nuts grown in the United States, an estimated $3 billion worth of crops ever year. Globally, bees pollinate about $24 billion worth of crops—almost 10 percent of the total value of food production worldwide. Besides pollinating food crops, in wild places, bees pollinate the plants and fruit trees that feed everything from songbirds to grizzly bears. They are a key part of the food chain, the chain of what eats what in the wild.

Some bees pollinate food crops on their own. Others work with humans to do the job. Commercial beekeepers raise honeybees in

Commercial beekeepers take honeybees to farms and orchards to pollinate food crops. With the job complete, these beekeepers pack up their hives.

wooden boxes and truck their hives from farm to farm to pollinate crops, starting in February and continuing through August. Beekeepers take honeybee hives to orange groves in Florida, almond orchards in California, and apple orchards in Indiana.

If you've ever carved a jack-o'-lantern or dined on pumpkin pie, you can thank squash bees (*Peponapis* and *Xenoglossa*). These bees get to work at dawn, right as pumpkin, squash, and zucchini blossoms are opening. Squash bees build their nests right under the plants they pollinate, so stroll through a pumpkin patch, and you'll be walking over nests of young squash bees.

If you prefer blueberries, be grateful for the southeastern blueberry bee (*Habropoda laboriosa*). This small, solitary creature is active for only a few weeks every year—right when blueberries bloom. In its short lifetime, a blueberry bee can visit fifty thousand

A blueberry bee visits a blueberry flower.

blueberry flowers and pollinate enough of them to create six thousand ripe blueberries, about thirty-five dollars' worth of fresh fruit. Blueberry bees are experts at buzz pollination, shaking loose the pollen from blueberry flowers with a high-pitched buzz.

If you love a wide range of fruit, consider the blue orchard bee (*Osmia lignaria*). About the size of honeybees but metallic blue-black, blue orchard bees pollinate cherries, pears, plums, peaches, apples, and almonds. They fly in all sorts of weather: cloudy days, rainy days, and the chilly days of early spring, all days when many other bees won't come out. The bee's unusual foraging technique virtually ensures the flower gets fertilized. The bee executes a "belly flop" onto a flower and "drags her hairy abdomen, mashing pollen into it, dropping pollen everywhere she goes," says Dave Hunter, founder of Crown Bees, a Washington State company that supplies bees to farmers and gardeners.

BEES MADE YOUR ICE CREAM

If you like cold, creamy ice cream, thank a bee. Bees pollinate alfalfa, a major food source for dairy cows. Without bees, there would be no alfalfa for cows to eat. So there would be no butter, no milk—and no ice cream.

Bees also help produce a wide range of ice cream flavors. If you like fruity flavors, remember that bees pollinate strawberries, blueberries, peaches, mangoes, and cherries. If you like some crunch on your cone, keep in mind that bees pollinate almonds, Brazil nuts, macadamia nuts, and cashews. If you prefer a little caffeine buzz, you'll want to know that bees pollinate coffee plants. Bees also pollinate the plants that give us vanilla.

But making one flavor is not their job. Bees do not make chocolate. The only pollinator of the cacao tree, *Theobroma cacao*, is a tiny fly known as the chocolate midge. Cacao tree flowers smell a little like mushrooms, a type of fungus, and these midges are ordinarily drawn to fungus. So the next time you take a delicious bite of chocolate ice cream, you can thank the chocolate midge.

Working together, all these bees keep the world's food supply going. A large study of pollination carried out by an international team of researchers and published in *Science* in 2013 showed that wild pollinators are essential for pollinating more than forty crops worldwide. Bees pollinate the foods that provide most of the vitamins and essential nutrients in our diet, including nearly all of our vitamin C. "If all the pollinators went extinct, we probably wouldn't starve," said University of California, Berkeley, biologist Claire Kremen. "But we'd all have scurvy [a disease caused by a lack of vitamin C] or some other vitamin-deficiency disorder."

A TASTE FOR HONEY

While some beekeepers raise honeybees to serve as pollinators on commercial farms, others raise honeybees for their honey. People have raised bees and collected their honey for thousands of years. But humans aren't the only ones who love honey. Honeybees eat it too.

To make honey, a honeybee drinks sugary nectar from flowers and stores it in its crop—an extra stomach. Chemicals produced in the crop convert the sugars in the nectar into honey. The honeybee then flies with its full crop back to its hive.

Back at the hive, other honeybees have created a honeycomb, a structure built of six-sided compartments, made of wax produced in the bees' bodies. The forager regurgitates the honey from its crop, which is watery at this stage, and deposits it into the cells of the honeycomb. Other honeybees fan the honeycomb with their wings, drying out the extra water. The bees then seal the comb with more wax. They will eat the stored honey during cold winter months, when flowers and nectar aren't available.

To look at what happens when wild bees disappear, take a springtime walk through a blossoming pear or apple orchard in Sichuan, China. For thousands of years, people in this fruit-growing region pollinated their trees the usual way: they let the bees do it. But in the 1980s, four decades of dousing the orchards with insect-killing pesticides also harmed the bees, causing the population of native bees to collapse. Without natural pollinators, farmers must pay workers to do the work that wild bees used to do for free. The workers climb ladders to scale the trees. They carry paintbrushes made of bamboo and chicken feathers and pots of pollen collected from flowers. Dipping their brushes into the

Using a small brush, a farmworker pollinates a squash flower. As bee populations decline, some farms must resort to hand-pollination.

pots, the workers hand-pollinate every blossom. They enlist their children to climb up to the highest blossoms.

"If we had to try and do what bees do on a daily basis, if we had to come out here and hand pollinate all of our native plants and our agricultural plants, there is physically no way we could do it," says North Carolina State University ecologist Rebecca Irwin. Chinese farmers can manage the task only when they have plenty of workers, but there are not enough people in the world to pollinate all our crops by hand. "Our best bet is to conserve our native bees," says Irwin.

Consider all that bees do for us, and you'll begin to understand why the decline of bees has set off alarm bells among scientists, conservationists, and world leaders. As the world's human population grows toward eight billion, the disappearance of bees could be devastating for people and lead to a global food crisis.

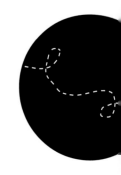

4

A Bee Cs

There are green bees and there are blue bees, and there's iridescence and stripes, and large ones and tiny ones.

—Sam Droege, bee researcher

Picture a bee. If you're like many people, the image that pops into your head is a honeybee or a bumblebee. But honeybees and bumblebees are just the tip of the bee iceberg. Honeybees and bumblebees make up just 1 percent of all the bees in the world. Of the 20,000 bee species, only 250 are bumblebees, and just 7 are honeybees.

What makes a bee a bee? Like all insects, bees have a three-part body plan: a head, a thorax, and an abdomen. On the head are a pair of large compound eyes, used for seeing color and objects. Each compound eye is made of thousands of single eyes, each pointing in a different direction. The pair of large compound eyes gives the bee a wide field of view. In the center of the head are three simple

A honeybee carries pollen in a corbicula, a basketlike structure on its legs.

eyes, used for sensing light intensity and the direction of the sun. Knowing where the sun is helps bees navigate. Bees have two long and sensitive antennae for touching and smelling. Strong mandibles, or jaws, bite and dig. A proboscis, or tongue, is for drinking nectar. Tongue length varies widely among bees. For instance, bumblebees have long tongues.

The middle body section is the thorax. A bee's six legs and two pairs of wings attach to the thorax. Bumblebees carry pollen on corbicula. Some kinds of bees have scopa on their legs, thoraxes, or abdomens. Most of the thorax has flight muscles, the muscles that control the wings.

The abdomen is the bee's rear section. It is divided into six segments in females and seven in males. The abdomen contains organs used for mating and egg laying.

A Bee Cs

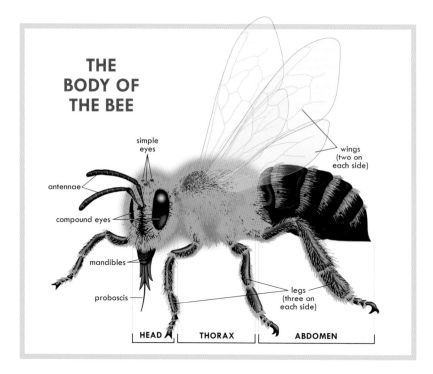

THE BODY OF THE BEE

simple eyes

antennae

compound eyes

mandibles

proboscis

wings (two on each side)

legs (three on each side)

| HEAD | THORAX | ABDOMEN |

Bee species vary from one to the next, in terms of size, wing shape, color, hairiness, and other features. But all bees have the same basic body structure.

VARIETY SHOW

Bees vary greatly in their lifestyles and behavior. Some sting when they are threatened or to defend their nests. Bumblebees and honeybees sting, but a great many bees don't.

All bees need nests to take care of their young. Some species nest in abandoned snail shells and others in hollow flower stems. Some species choose dried cow dung. Nesting material also varies from species to species, from wax the bees make themselves to pebbles mixed with tree sap or pieces of leaves. Cuckoo bees do not build nests at all but sneak their eggs into the nests of other bees. The world of bees is wide and varied.

Sam Droege heads the US Geological Survey's Native Bee Inventory and Monitoring Program in Maryland. When Droege heard that native pollinators could be in trouble, he picked up a camera and began pointing his lens on wild bees. He has taken

BEE OR NOT A BEE?

You hear a buzz and spot an insect. Is it a bee? Not always.

People often mistake wasps for bees, since the two are closely related. But there are easy ways to tell them apart: most bees are hairy and their bodies are rounded. Wasps tend to be hairless with thinner waists. Some bees "look like cotton candy with wings," writes Joseph S. Wilson and Olivia Messinger Carril, authors of *The Bees in Your Backyard: A Guide to North American Bees.* Wasps "look like Olympic swimmers, devoid of all hair, skinny-waisted, and with long spindly legs." If the insect is carrying pollen on its body or back legs, it's a bee, not a wasp.

People sometimes mistake certain flies for bees. Bee flies (*Bombylius*) and flower flies (Syrphidae) visit flowers, just as bees do. They have hairy, striped bodies as bees do. By looking like bees, these harmless insects fool predators such as birds into thinking they can sting.

To tell a bee from a fly, look at the wings. Flies have two, and bees have four. But be sure to look closely. Bees can hook each pair of wings together, making it appear as if they have two wings instead of four. If you can't tell from the wings, check the eyes. Fly eyes are huge and sit perched on top of the head, while bees have smaller eyes that rest on the sides of the head. Finally, you can inspect the antennae. Flies have short antennae, while bees sport long ones.

thousands of very detailed, high-definition shots of North American bees to help researchers better identify native bees. And his pictures might surprise you. "Everyone knows what a bee is," says Droege. "And they have a mind picture of something that looks kind of like a honeybee, maybe a little more colorful. And then you show them these pictures. And there are green bees and there are blue bees, and there's iridescence and stripes, and large ones and tiny ones."

A Bee Cs

CUCKOO BEES

Cuckoo bees are parasites, organisms that take advantage of other organisms to survive. Cuckoo bees take advantage of other bees. They lay their eggs in the nests of other bees and trick these bees into raising their young. Because they don't need to feed their own young, many cuckoo bees have lost adaptations, such as hairy bodies, that allow them to collect pollen. Some are nearly hairless and look a lot like wasps.

In early spring, you may see them flying low over the ground, searching for nests of other bee species. Once a female cuckoo bee finds a nest, she waits nearby. Then, while the rightful owner of the nest is off searching for food, she sneaks in and lays her eggs. The busy nest owner thinks the eggs are its own and raises the cuckoo bee's larvae when they hatch. Cuckoo bees tend to hatch early and eat the food of the host bee's larvae. The mother cuckoo bee or her larvae may even kill the other bee's larvae. The advantage for cuckoo bees is that they are freeloaders. They don't have to build their own nest or raise their own young.

He posts the photos online and makes them freely available to anyone who wants to print them, publish them, or share them online. Bee researchers rely on them to identify little-known species. Other people use them to marvel at the extraordinary diversity thrumming in our backyards.

Bees come in all colors, shapes, and sizes. The world's smallest may be *Perdita minima* from the southwestern United States. It can hardly be seen without a magnifying lens. At less than 0.08 inches (0.2 cm) long, it is about the size of a gnat. The world's biggest lives in Indonesia, and it is Wallace's giant bee (*Megachile pluto*). With a body 1.5 inches (3.8 cm) long and a wingspan of 2.5 inches (6.3 cm), it is nearly twenty times the size of *Perdita minima*.

Bee photos from Sam
Droege's collection

Mining bees are solitary bees. They make their nests in holes in the ground.

Bees can be social, living together and sharing the work of raising the young. Or they can be solitary, living and rearing their young alone. Most bees—about 90 percent—are solitary. A solitary female builds her nest and gathers all the food needed for her young before they are born. She builds her nest, loads it with pollen and eggs (her unborn young), and then dies. Her offspring emerge from their eggs, feed on the pollen she has left for them, and grow into adults. Adult males mate with adult females, and shortly after mating, the males die. The females then prepare new nests, fill them with pollen, lay their eggs, and then die. The cycle continues with the next generation.

The remaining 10 percent of bees are social. The most well-known social bees are honeybees and bumblebees. They live in colonies with a queen (a fertile female whose job is to lay eggs) and female workers, who divide the chores of feeding and caring for the young. But honeybees and bumblebees differ in important ways. Honeybees live in large colonies that survive from year to year. In bumblebee colonies, almost every bee in the colony dies before winter. Only the new queen survives.

THE REMARKABLE, HARDWORKING HUMBLEBEE

Bumblebees—humblebees or dumbledors, as they were known in England a couple of hundred years ago—are hardworking pollinators. They use buzz pollination and can control their own body temperature. So they collect pollen even in cold weather.

Most insects are cold-blooded—their body temperature matches the temperature of the surrounding air. But bumblebees have the ability to warm their bodies. To prepare for flights in cool weather, they vibrate their flight muscles to warm themselves. Their chubby bodies and thick fur also help them stay warm. On cool days, these plump, fuzzy workhorses collect pollen when many other kinds of bees are home safe in their nests. Because bumblebees can warm themselves, they are able to live in cold places— alpine meadows, windy prairies, and northern forests. This makes them vital to reproduction of the plants and animals that live in those places. One type of bumblebee even resides in the Arctic— the northernmost region on Earth.

Bombus polaris, an Arctic bumblebee, feeds on salvia flowers in the spring. Some bumblebees are adapted to live in cold places.

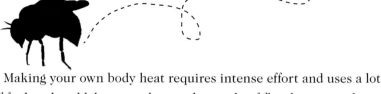

Making your own body heat requires intense effort and uses a lot of fuel, so bumblebees need a steady supply of floral nectar—the insect equivalent of an energy drink. If a bumblebee is able to find flowers and fuel up, it fires up its flight muscles—and off it goes.

THE BUMBLEBEE YEAR

Life for a bumblebee colony begins in early spring. As the snow melts and the soil warms, the queen emerges from a hole in the ground. She flies slowly over the ground, sweeping in a side-to-side motion as she searches for a place to build her nest. If she finds a promising spot, like an abandoned rodent hole or a crevice in a stack of firewood, she climbs inside and explores. Once she chooses a nest site, she readies it for her offspring. She makes the nest snug by lining it with feathers, hair, dried moss, or grass. She secretes wax from glands in her abdomen and molds it with her legs into a thimble-sized cup, called a honey pot. She forages for nectar and pollen from spring flowers, returns to her nest, and fills the wax cup with a lump of pollen moistened with nectar.

She is then ready to lay her eggs. As the eggs pass out of her body, she fertilizes them with sperm stored inside of her from mating with a male the year before. The size of the clutch, or batch of eggs, varies. A typical clutch is eight or sixteen eggs, depending on the species of bumblebee. The queen pushes the cream-colored eggs into the lump of pollen and seals the tiny cup with more wax. Then, like a bird, she incubates her eggs, resting her abdomen over them to keep them warm. As she sits, she eats from another honey pot kept close by.

Sometimes she leaves the nest to find more food for herself, but it's a careful balancing act. "If a bumblebee runs out of energy, she cannot fly," explains bumblebee expert Dave Goulson, an entomologist at the University of Sussex in England. "And if she cannot fly, she cannot get to flowers to get more food." But if she stays away too long, her eggs will get cold, will develop too slowly, and may die. The colony needs plenty of nectar-rich spring flowers nearby. Even slight changes in the availability of food can have big effects on the success of the colony. If flowers are too few and far apart, she will have to forage farther from the nest and she risks running out of fuel. Says Goulson, "A bumblebee with a full stomach is only ever about forty minutes from starvation."

In a few days, the eggs hatch into soft, white larvae. Each larva is shaped like a tiny sausage. It has no eyes and no legs, but it does have a giant mouth, which makes a lot of sense. A bee larva is an eating machine. It does nothing but graze on the pollen and nectar left by its mother. As it grows, it molts, or sheds its skin. Then, like a moth or butterfly, it spins a silken cocoon around itself and changes into a pupa. Inside the cocoon, its internal parts dissolve and the body rebuilds itself into the form of an adult bee. Nearly four weeks after it began its life as an egg, the bee chews its way out of the cocoon and emerges as an adult.

The first adults to emerge are the female workers, the queen's daughters. They are entirely white when they emerge. "With a little imagination," says Goulson, they resemble "rather cuddly miniature polar bears." Within a few days, they lose their white color and take on the black-and-yellow colors of mature bumblebees. They take over foraging and housekeeping duties so the queen can stay inside the nest and lay eggs. The colony grows rapidly, with more and more female workers emerging from their cocoons. By the end of summer, the colony may number a few hundred workers. In late summer or early fall, the queen lays more eggs, but these are different. First, she lays a clutch of unfertilized eggs. They are males, also called drones. Then she lays a clutch of fertilized eggs. These are females, but they don't become workers. They become new queens. The males find and mate with as many new queens as possible, setting the stage for the next generation of bees.

THE TRUTH ABOUT STINGS

Among bee species that sting, such as bumblebees and honeybees, only the females can sting. Few native bee species sting, and you have to be very rough with bees or threaten their nests for them to sting you. Many native bees can't sting at all.

Only worker honeybees have barbed stings that catch in the skin. Once a worker honeybee stings the flesh of an attacker, it can't pull the stinger back out. The stinger is torn from its body, and the bee soon dies. Honeybees are some of the most aggressive stingers, using stinging as a way to defend their hives, and their stings are quite painful. In bumblebees and other native bees, the stinger is smooth, not barbed, so it slides out of the victim's flesh.

For most people, a beesting isn't serious, causing temporary pain, redness, and swelling at the site. But for people who are allergic to bee venom, a sting can cause a life-threatening reaction. Those people should always carry an epinephrine auto-injector, a medical device that treats allergic reactions.

When winter comes, every single bumblebee dies except the new queens. Each newly mated queen finds a winter hideaway, climbs inside, and sleeps until spring.

 ## HIVE AND SEEK

When many people hear the word *bee*, they think of honeybees. Formally known as the European honeybee, or *Apis mellifera,* this tan-colored bee lives in hives with a single queen, tens of thousands of female workers, and several hundred drones. Honeybees are not native to North America. They arrived on the continent around 1620 when colonists from England sailed with their hives across

Honeybees build honeycombs, where they store honey and where the queen bee lays her eggs.

the Atlantic Ocean. Some of these honeybees escaped from their human-controlled hives and lived in the wild. Entomologists use the word *naturalized* to refer to these escaped bees. *Naturalized* means "not native." They live in the wild alongside true native bees.

Unlike bumblebee colonies, honeybee colonies survive the winter. A queen and her workers (all female) build durable, long-lasting honeycombs from wax secreted from glands on their abdomens. Domesticated bees (those kept by humans) typically nest in wooden boxes provided by beekeepers. Wild honeybees usually build their nests in hollow trees.

A honeybee colony is much larger than a bumblebee colony. A honeybee colony may have thirty thousand to fifty thousand bees, including a single queen and several hundred drones. During the cold winter months, the queen doesn't lay eggs and her workers don't forage. They cluster around the queen and form a honeybee huddle. The worker bees point their heads inward and shiver their muscles, which generates heat. With thousands of bees all shivering at once, the hive stays pleasantly warm, even in cold weather. When workers on the outer edge of the huddle get cold, they push toward

A Bee Cs

HONEYBEE LIFE STAGES

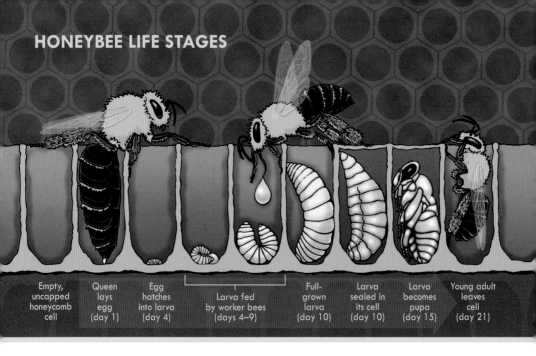

Empty, uncapped honeycomb cell	Queen lays egg (day 1)	Egg hatches into larva (day 4)	Larva fed by worker bees (days 4–9)	Full-grown larva (day 10)	Larva sealed in its cell (day 10)	Larva becomes pupa (day 15)	Young adult leaves cell (day 21)

After a queen honeybee lays eggs (one per cell), they hatch into larvae. Nurse bees care for the newly hatched larvae. Then larvae spin cocoons, becoming pupae, and finally emerge as adult bees.

the center and other bees take a turn on the outside. The colony survives on honey made and stored earlier in the year, when flowers were in bloom and nectar was plentiful.

When spring arrives and flowers begin to bloom once more, workers go out foraging and the queen begins to lay eggs. She lays each egg inside a six-sided wax cell in a honeycomb. Fertilized eggs will become workers, and unfertilized eggs will become drones. When these eggs hatch into larvae, the youngest worker bees, called nurse bees, care for them in their cells. For the first two days, nurse bees secrete a substance called royal jelly from glands on their heads and feed it to the growing larva. After that, they feed the larvae a mixture of pollen and honey called beebread. After about six days, the workers cap each cell with more wax, sealing each larva inside. Each larva spins a cocoon and changes into a pupa. About a week or two later, the adult bee emerges from its cell.

A young worker bee begins her life as a nurse, taking care of larvae. As she grows older, she begins to perform other hive chores, such as cleaning out empty cells. Eventually, she learns to make honey and scout for pollen and nectar. When a scout finds food, she carries a sample of it back to the hive. She tells the other worker bees where to find it by performing a waggle dance. She runs in a straight line while waggling her abdomen and then circles back. The direction and speed of her dance tell her sisters where the food is in relation to the sun and how good the food source is. The workers then fly out to find the food. Each worker honeybee can carry half her weight in pollen and nectar back to the hive. This food is fed to larvae or stored as honey.

In spring or summer, if the hive becomes too crowded, the old queen leaves the hive and takes about half of her workers to build a new hive. The workers begin to raise a new queen by feeding several larvae large amounts of royal jelly. The first of the new queens to emerge kills the other queens and then leaves to mate with nearby drones from other colonies. The drones die after mating. The newly fertilized queen returns to the hive, where she begins to lay eggs.

The life span varies for each type of honeybee. A worker bee may live for a few weeks up to a year. A queen lives longer, typically two to four years. Drones live for a few weeks or months and die upon mating. When winter approaches and food becomes scarce, workers force any unmated male bees out of the nest. These unmated drones will die from cold and starvation. Meanwhile, the rest of the hive prepares to face the lean winter months ahead.

5

Disease
Spillover

When we try to pick out anything by itself, we find it
hitched to everything else in the universe.

—John Muir, naturalist

When reports from Robbin Thorp and others about possible
declines of North American bumblebees began piling up in the first
decade of the twenty-first century, bee scientists were abuzz. But
University of Illinois entomologist Sydney Cameron wondered if
bumblebees truly were in decline across North America. "People
were just making these wide-ranging declarations about bumblebee
decline around the United States, and then making guesses about
why," she said. No one had carried out a scientific survey of North
American bumblebees.

So Cameron teamed up with Jamie Strange, a US Department of
Agriculture entomologist, to investigate. They chose eight North
American bumblebee species. All had once been common, but four

had *appeared* to become rare in the last few decades. Had they really declined?

In 2007 and 2009, Cameron, Strange, and their coworkers traveled to forty US states. They netted and killed more than sixteen thousand bumblebees and brought them back to the lab to identify. Then they combed through museum collections, looking at bumblebees in drawers and back rooms, going a hundred years back. The team counted the nearly seventy-four thousand museum bees and verified the identity of each species and the catch location. Then they compared the two sets of bumblebees.

They found that the four species thought to be declining had become rarer. The western bumblebee, for example, made up 20 percent of bees in museum collections but only 1 percent of bees collected in the field. The American bumblebee (*Bombus pensylvanicus*) and the yellow-banded bumblebee had also become scarce. But the bee that had declined the most was the rusty patched bumblebee, which had plummeted by 96 percent. The remaining four species showed no overall decline.

Disease Spillover

The team could make a few conclusions. The culprit didn't appear to be some general bee killer, such as a pesticide, since some North American bumblebee species appeared to be doing fine. The killer also wasn't something specific to one place, since bumblebees were disappearing all over the continent. Whatever the killer was, it was hitting many close relatives of Franklin's bumblebee and hitting them all at once all over the country.

The next step would be to nail down the cause. Thorp and Cameron shared a hunch. They thought it had something to do with bumblebee factories.

 ## BUMBLEBEES AT WORK

Along the Pacific coast, in the town of Delta, British Columbia, the sun glints off a vast commercial greenhouse. The glass behemoth sprawls across 45 acres (18 ha)—about the size of thirty-four football fields. This is Windset Farms, a grower of premium tomatoes, peppers, and cucumbers for supermarkets throughout North America and around the world.

On the door, a sign reads, "Caution: Bumblebees at work."

Inside, in the warm and humid air, row upon row of tomato vines rise out of white tanks and climb on strings suspended from the high ceiling. Among the rows sit stacks of cardboard boxes. They look like boxes that might hold reams of office paper. But these boxes have bees buzzing inside them.

From a small hole in one of the boxes, a worker bumblebee pokes out her head. She climbs out and flies to a cluster of yellow flowers on a tomato plant. She is a commercial bumblebee, raised in a factory and shipped here for the job of pollinating tomatoes. Thousands more like her are busy at work. Without the bees, tomato production at greenhouses like this one would stop.

So the next time you squirt ketchup on your fries or dip a corn chip into a jar of salsa, take a moment to reflect on the hardworking

An employee at a vegetable greenhouse in Germany opens a box of bees. The insects pollinate tomato plants there.

bumblebee. A bumblebee pollinated the flower that produced the tomato that became ketchup and salsa. Every tomato you have ever eaten—whether grown in a pot on a patio, on a farm, or in a vast commercial greenhouse—was almost certainly pollinated by a bumblebee.

 ## THE BUZZINESS OF BUMBLEBEES

Bumblebees didn't always work in greenhouses. Until the mid-1980s, teams of workers used to pollinate greenhouse tomatoes by hand. They walked up and down the rows and touched each flower with a vibrating wand. The vibration released the pollen, which drifted into the air and landed on the flower's female reproductive organs. It was slow, costly work. In 1985 Belgian veterinarian and bumblebee lover Roland De Jonghe found a new way. He placed a nest of bumblebees in a greenhouse full of tomatoes. It worked. The bees pollinated all the tomatoes, eliminating the need for teams of workers with their vibrating wands.

In 1987 De Jonghe founded the first company to raise commercial bumblebees. Other European companies soon joined the bumblebee business. In 1989 they began shipping bees to greenhouses in Holland, France, and the United Kingdom. Next came Canada, the United States, Israel, Morocco, and Japan. By 2016 companies were shipping two million bumblebee colonies per year to countries all over the world.

"Bumblebee factories" are secretive operations. British biologist Dave Goulson is one of the few outsiders who has been allowed inside. "The scale of the operations is staggering," he reports. "Imagine vast white rooms the size of [soccer fields], with tall stacked ranks of bumblebee nests on shelves in row after row stretching into the distance, tended by teams of technicians in white lab coats sweating in the warm, sticky conditions."

Any new technology carries risks, and bumblebee factories are no exception. A big risk is the spread of disease. Bumblebees suffer from a witches' brew of ailments, and the mass-rearing of bumblebees in factories provides an incubator for those diseases to spread. When bumblebees started to decline across North America, researchers became suspicious about commercial bumblebees. They suspected that these bees were spreading diseases to populations of bees in the wild, with devastating effects.

 ## "RIDDLED WITH DISEASES"

It is a universal law of disease transmission: infections can spread readily through a crowded population. Think of how a runny nose or cough can race around a kindergarten classroom. Just as those kindergarteners often carry their germs home with them, infecting their families, diseased bumblebees carry their illnesses with them.

Bumblebee factories try hard to prevent diseases. Workers clean and disinfect the facilities. They regularly screen bees for diseases. They destroy nests that house sick bees.

Even so, when scientists have tested the nests from these bumblebee factories, often they have found them heavily infected. "Despite the extensive precautions used in the factories," Goulson said, "their bumblebees are riddled with diseases."

What happens when diseased bumblebees escape into the wild? And with millions of nests shipped around the world, some bumblebees escape. Some escape through greenhouse vents. More escape through the greenhouse door when people go in and out. Or they escape through broken greenhouse windows.

That's how pathogens (disease-carrying agents) from commercial bees spill over into a wild population. If a commercial bee forages on a flower outside a greenhouse, it can pass any diseases it carries to its wild relatives. In recent decades, parasitic mites carried by European bumblebees have shown up in Japan and attacked Japanese bumblebees. In Chile and Argentina, the only bumblebee native to southern South America has declined rapidly. The culprit in each case is disease spillover from commercial bumblebees. But the most alarming case of disease spillover may be playing out in North America.

 ## SUSPICIOUS TIMING

In the 1990s, the Animal and Plant Health Inspection Service, a division of the US Department of Agriculture, banned the importing of European bees into the United States. The inspection service is in charge of keeping out plants and animals that might spread diseases to US crops and livestock. Since they could no longer ship bees to the United States, European bumblebee companies set up factories in the United States and raised two native American species, the common eastern bumblebee (*Bombus impatiens*) and the western bumblebee. The eastern bumblebee went to work at

Disease Spillover

greenhouses in the East and the western bumblebee to greenhouses in the West.

Then things got a little complicated. One of the European companies wanted to raise North American bumblebees in its factories in Belgium. The inspection service agreed. So from 1992 to 1994, companies shipped North American queens across the Atlantic Ocean, reared them in European factories alongside European bumblebees, and then shipped their nests—containing queens and their offspring—back to the United States for use in US greenhouses. Did those native American bees, raised in European factories, bring a foreign disease home with them?

Then came more complications. In 1997 disease broke out in a bumblebee factory in California. *Nosema bombi*, a fungus that lives in the guts of bumblebees, raged through factories full of western bumblebees, killing all the commercial bees. No treatment existed for the fungus, leaving growers with no way to get rid of it. Robbin Thorp learned about the outbreak at a scientific symposium, right before he began monitoring Franklin's bumblebee. The problem grew so bad that companies eventually gave up on the western bumblebee for commercial use. But they stuck with the eastern bumblebee and shipped it to greenhouses all over the United States.

Several years later, when Thorp observed sharp declines of Franklin's bumblebee in the wild, he thought about commercial bumblebees. He thought about native bees being shipped across the Atlantic, raised in European factories, and sent back home, along with their offspring. He thought about the disease outbreak in the California factory. He hypothesized (developed an idea for further investigation) that commercial bumblebees were escaping into the wild and passing a disease to their wild relatives. His hypothesis would explain why only some North American bumblebees were in decline. The ones disappearing were closely related, and Thorp hypothesized that they were the most susceptible to *Nosema bombi*.

Other researchers, including Sydney Cameron, agreed that the timing was suspicious. The disappearance of Franklin's and other bumblebees came shortly after commercial bumblebees came to North America. But was it truly cause and effect, or was it a coincidence? Had greenhouse bees spread diseases to wild bees?

PIECING TOGETHER THE PUZZLE

Researchers began investigating Thorp's idea that diseases were spilling over from greenhouse bees into populations of wild bees. Michael Otterstatter and a team of scientists at the University of Toronto filled in one piece of the puzzle. They tramped into fields and collected two sets of bumblebees: those foraging near commercial greenhouses and those foraging far away from greenhouses. (As they were out collecting bees, the team saw for themselves commercial bumblebees entering and leaving greenhouses through vents.) The team brought both sets of bees back to the lab and tested them for four pathogens, including *Nosema bombi*.

Bees from greenhouses can spread disease to bees living in the wild.

They found that bees collected near greenhouses had much higher rates of disease than those collected far from greenhouses. They were more likely to have *Nosema bombi,* and the infections were more intense. Infection rates were lower and infections milder in bees collected far from greenhouses. Another disease, *Crithidia bombi,* was found only in bees near greenhouses. It really did look as if diseases were spilling out of greenhouses.

Sydney Cameron and Jamie Strange added another piece of the puzzle. When their team had carried out their survey of eight North American bumblebee species and netted more than sixteen thousand bees in the field, they examined those bees for the presence of *Nosema bombi.* Of the eight species, four had stable populations and four had declining populations. Cameron's team found that the four declining species all had high rates of *Nosema bombi.* The four stable species all had low levels of infection. "The conclusions that we drew from the screening of *Nosema,*" said Cameron "was that indeed there was a very significant correlation between the declining species and the high prevalence of *Nosema bombi.*"

Cameron and other scientists thought that a new European strain of *Nosema bombi* had entered the United States and Canada via North American bumblebees raised in European factories. The native bumblebees might have been unable to fight off this foreign strain. To test this idea, Cameron examined bumblebees dating back one hundred years, the bees they had found in drawers and back rooms of museums. Cameron and her colleagues tested the museum bees by looking for *Nosema bombi* DNA. Their tool was polymerase chain reaction, a simple laboratory test that can find a tiny bit of DNA and copy it repeatedly. The scientists looked for signs of *Nosema bombi* in the reproduced DNA of the museum specimens. Cameron knew that if she found no *Nosema bombi* in the museum bees, this would mean that the infection was new to North America and was likely coming from Europe.

CORRELATION OR CAUSATION?

Rates of infection with a parasite in wild bumblebees begin to rise. At the same time, wild bumblebee populations begin to fall. It would be easy to conclude that the parasite is what's killing the bees. But wait. Do we really know that the parasite is the cause?

Often a research study finds that two events, A and B, correlate, or occur together in a consistent way, and that chance alone can't explain it. But this doesn't mean that event A *caused* event B. It's also possible that event B caused event A. Or maybe a third change, event C, causes both events.

Suppose a change in the environment, such as a new pesticide (event C), is weakening bees' immune systems—the systems that fight off infection. With their immune systems weakened, bees are more likely to become infected with parasites (event A) and more likely to die from the infection (event B). In this example, event C is the real cause of plummeting bumblebee populations. Event A (the parasite infection) didn't cause event B (the falling population). Rather, event C caused both A and B. This explains why A and B always occur together: the same thing causes them.

Because it's easy to mistake correlation for causation, scientists are careful when they discuss their results. This is why they make statements like "event A and event B show a *strong correlation*" rather than "event A *causes* event B."

When you're reading about scientific studies, try to think like a scientist. Ask yourself, Does the study show causation? Or does it show correlation? If the answer is causation, challenge yourself to think about what else might explain those results.

But Cameron did find *Nosema bombi* in the museum collections—even in bees collected one hundred years earlier. So the infection was not new to North America. However, Cameron and her team uncovered another important clue. They learned

Disease Spillover

that although the fungus had been present in North America for a century, the infection rate had been very low in the past. Infection rates in native bumblebees began to jump in the 1990s—about when bumblebee commercialization took off.

 ## TOO FAT TO FLY?

If *Nosema bombi* was indeed the culprit, how exactly was it causing bumblebee declines? Jamie Strange has been trying to answer this question. He has been trying to figure out exactly how the pathogen affects the western bumblebee.

He has discovered that when *Nosema bombi* takes root in a colony, the males are hardest hit. "The males become really, really infected," he said. "Their abdomens become distended [swollen] from having all these spores of this fungus. In many cases they can't really fly, and those that can fly, can't fly for very long."

Strange thinks that infection could interrupt mating. His hypothesis is that an infected male, with its abdomen swollen, can't fly off to find a queen to mate with. Or perhaps it can't mate with a queen once it has found one. And without mating, next year's colony falls apart. A queen bumblebee can lay male offspring without her eggs being fertilized. But she can lay females only after she has mated. And since females do all the work of maintaining the colony, without females, the colony starves.

Strange is having a hard time proving his theory. The problem is that his team can't find western bumblebees that are free of the disease. Every nest they collect from the wild for their experiments is infected. Without a supply of *Nosema*-free western bumblebees, they can't run a controlled experiment—one that would enable them to compare infected bees with uninfected bees. "That's been our biggest challenge," he said, "getting clean [healthy] bees."

Other questions remain. One of the most puzzling is, If native American bumblebees have been exposed to *Nosema bombi*

RISKY BUZZINESS

Bee scientists have been advocating for better regulation of the commercial bumblebee business. They say the government regulations in place are not adequate to minimize the risks of disease spillover. They say some steps are needed: halting the shipment of bees outside their native ranges, improved screening for a wider range of pathogens within bumblebee factories, improved hygiene to eliminate pathogens within bumblebee factories, and improved barriers on greenhouses to avoid mixing of managed bees and wild bees.

"Bumblebees are marvelous pollinators and I really wouldn't want to see the industry come to a halt," says Robbin Thorp. "But I would like to see a lot more protection of the potential environmental risk."

for decades—as was demonstrated by screening the museum collections—what changed in the 1990s to cause infection rates to spike?

Different scientists have different ideas. Some scientists wonder whether modern bumblebees are more susceptible to the fungus because they have a virus that is weakening their ability to fight off other diseases. Some think bumblebees are more susceptible because other changes to the environment, such as loss of wildflowers, weaken them. Bumblebees depend on a steady diet of pollen and nectar from flowers blooming from spring until fall. But wildflower populations are shrinking. Urban and suburban development is gobbling up land, farms are growing bigger, and the use of plant-killing pesticides is on the rise. That means fewer wildflowers and less pollen and nectar for bumblebees to eat.

Strange and Cameron are investigating another possibility—whether bees become more susceptible to *Nosema* when they are exposed to a common pesticide, a chemical that kills insects.

Disease Spillover

EMPTY NESTERS

In 2006 Pennsylvania-based commercial beekeeper David Hackenberg, who was overwintering his honeybees in Florida, noticed that some of his beehives were nearly empty. Most of the worker honeybees had flown away from the hives and not returned, leaving behind the queen, immature bees, and a few nurse bees to care for the young. By 2007 beekeepers in thirty-three states and Canada were reporting the same thing: large numbers of their worker bees had vanished. Soon scientists named the problem colony collapse disorder (CCD).

David Hackenberg, owner of Hackenberg Apiaries in Lewisburg, Pennsylvania, was the first beekeeper to identify colony collapse disorder. This photo shows him with newly born honeybees in 2007.

Scientists began to investigate and uncovered a few clues. They learned that the mysterious disorder was mainly striking commercial honeybees. They learned that the honeybee hives most affected were shipped from place to place to pollinate crops. Hackenberg trucked his hives to six states: Florida, California, Georgia, Pennsylvania, Maine, and New York.

Then, as suddenly as it began, CCD seemed to disappear. The mysterious disorder peaked in 2007 and then faded. The particular pattern of CCD—worker bees mysteriously vanishing without a trace—itself vanished.

As of 2019, the cause of CCD remained a mystery. Scientists who investigated CCD had found no single cause. Most research pointed to a combination of factors including these:

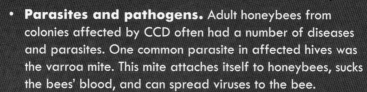

- **Parasites and pathogens.** Adult honeybees from colonies affected by CCD often had a number of diseases and parasites. One common parasite in affected hives was the varroa mite. This mite attaches itself to honeybees, sucks the bees' blood, and can spread viruses to the bee.
- **Poor diet.** Honeybees depend on nectar and pollen gathered from a variety of flowers. Research indicates that poor diet can weaken honeybees' immune systems and make them more susceptible to diseases. Commercial honeybees kept for long periods on farms with only one crop may have an impoverished diet.
- **Pesticides.** Pesticides sprayed on crops or sprayed on hives to control varroa mites and other pests can harm honeybees. Some research shows that pesticides can weaken honeybees' defenses or impair their ability to navigate, causing them to get lost on their way back to the hive.

Researchers who studied CCD think the factors tended to overlap and interact with one another. For example, pesticides or poor diet could have weakened some honeybees, making them more susceptible to disease.

Although beekeepers still report honeybee losses, those cases do not fit the pattern of CCD. Despite early worries that CCD could wipe out honeybees, the number of honeybee hives in the United States remained stable from 2006 to 2016 (the most recent year for which data were available).

Although CCD may have gone away, the mysterious disorder has had a lasting impact. It has shown the importance of pollinators to our food supply. "The silver lining of CCD," says Scott Black of the Xerces Society for Invertebrate [animals without backbones] Conservation, "is [that it] got people to look at pollinators and pollination."

6

The Day the Bees Died

If we were to wipe out insects alone, just that group alone, on this planet . . . the rest of life and humanity with it would mostly disappear from the land. And within a few months.

—E. O. Wilson, biologist

It was Pollinator Week 2013, a time in June set aside to celebrate the valuable role of butterflies, beetles, birds, bats and, of course, bees. The offices were bustling at the Xerces Society for Invertebrate Conservation in Portland, Oregon, an organization devoted to insect conservation. Staff members were busy fielding inquiries from gardeners and others: *What bee is this? Can you recommend the best flowers for my garden?* Then the phone started ringing. Caller after caller reported seeing dead bees—lots of dead bees.

Staff members rushed to the scene: a suburban shopping center in Wilsonville, Oregon. In the parking lot, dead bees clung to blossoms on the linden trees. Thousands more dead bees littered

A French beekeeper holds dead bees that were poisoned by pesticides.

the pavement under the trees. More dead bees were falling from the branches with each passing minute. Most of the dead were bumblebees.

Workers rushed to wrap the trees with bee-proof netting. This would keep more bumblebees from reaching the trees and dying. Even so, the death toll was severe. About fifty thousand bumblebees died that day.

"SOMEBODY REALLY SCREWED UP"

The incident in Wilsonville was the largest wild bee kill ever recorded. Scientists estimated that the bumblebee deaths that day dealt a devastating blow to three hundred more bumblebee colonies.

In response to the bee deaths, the Oregon Department of Agriculture investigated. Its staffers tested the trees and the bodies of dead bees, and concluded that the bees had died from a pesticide. A landscaping company had applied the pesticide

The Day the Bees Died

to fifty blooming linden trees in the parking lot to kill aphids. These tiny sap-sucking insects feed by sucking juices from plant stems and leaves. As the insects feed, they leave behind a sticky residue called honeydew. In the Wilsonville parking lot, the honeydew had dripped onto the pavement and parked cars below. To prevent this nuisance, the parking lot manager had arranged to spray the trees.

But linden tree blossoms are also a magnet for bumblebees, and when they landed on the trees, the pesticide killed them. Investigators concluded that the application of the pesticide on blooming linden trees was a violation of the product's directions. The product label clearly stated that the pesticide is toxic to bees and that it should not be sprayed on plants in bloom when bees were visiting. "This is a big mistake," Mace Vaughan of the Xerces Society told a television news reporter that day. "Somebody really screwed up." After the bee kill that day, the Oregon Department of Agriculture confirmed six more bee kills caused by the application to trees of a new type of pesticide called neonicotinoids, or neonics for short.

 ## "A SPRING WITHOUT VOICES"

Bees are beneficial insects. They pollinate the world's plants and help produce the food we need. But some insects are pests, particularly on farms. They eat or destroy the crops that farmers are trying to grow. Pests can invade our homes, spread diseases, or simply be a nuisance—like the aphids that were dripping sticky honeydew in the Wilsonville parking lot.

People have been farming for ten thousand years, and they've been battling insect pests on their crops just as long. In the twentieth century, newly developed chemical pesticides became a new tool in their arsenal. A pesticide is a chemical that kills or repels a pest, especially an insect. People spray pesticides to control insects on farms, in homes and gardens, in schools, and in workplaces. In 2012 (the most recent year for which data is available) US farmers applied 34 million pounds (15 million kg) of pesticides to control insect pests on their crops. Another 26 million pounds (12 million kg) of pesticides were used in US homes, schools, government buildings, and businesses. The battle of the bugs has become an all-out war. Yet pesticides often harm other living things, not just pests.

To prevent insect damage to crops, farmers spray pesticides. But pesticides can also kill helpful insects, such as bees.

One of the first people to sound the alarm about pesticides was American biologist and author Rachel Carson. In her 1962 book *Silent Spring*, she laid out the perils of pesticides and warned of "a spring without voices," one in which no birds sang, in which "no bees droned among the blossoms." Her prophecy of birds and insects killed—and people sickened—by pesticides alarmed the American public. The book changed the way farmers, citizens, and lawmakers thought about pesticides and their role in the environment. It helped lead to the creation of the US Environmental Protection Agency (EPA). Established in 1970, this US agency is charged with protecting human health and the environment.

Biologist Rachel Carson sounded the alarm about the dangers of pesticides in the 1960s. In her book *Silent Spring*, she called the public's attention to the hazards of using these dangerous chemicals.

When *Silent Spring* was published, organophosphates were among the most widely used pesticides in the world. These pesticides are highly effective against insect pests. But they also happen to be highly toxic, affecting the nervous system of humans, birds, and other animals. "They're considered junior-strength nerve agents because they have the same mechanism of action as nerve gases like sarin [a chemical weapon]," says Dana Boyd Barr, a scientist at Emory University in Atlanta, Georgia, who has studied organophosphate poisoning. At high levels, they can kill people and wildlife.

Another group of pesticides widely used in Carson's time included dichloro-diphenyl-trichloroethane (DDT) and similar compounds. DDT builds up in the fatty tissues of exposed animals. As one animal eats another, DDT moves up the food chain, from insects to mice, fish, and frogs and then to animals that eat them, such as birds of prey (for example, eagles, hawks, and condors).

DDT harms wild birds by thinning their eggshells. In the nest, the thin eggshells can't support the weight of a mother or father bird and break beneath them, killing the developing offspring. The widespread use of DDT led to the decline of bald eagles and other birds of prey in the United States. And although DDT is less acutely toxic to mammals than organophosphates are, it likely causes cancer in people. Opposition to DDT grew, largely because of Carson's *Silent Spring*, and the United States banned the pesticide in 1972.

With all the problems with these pesticides, the EPA and other groups sought less toxic alternatives. By the 1990s, researchers had developed a new class of pesticides that was much less toxic to people, birds, and other animals.

 ## "SILVER BULLETS THAT MISFIRED"

This new class, neonicotinoids, is based on nicotine, the natural chemical found in tobacco plants. Neonics kill insect pests by blocking nerve impulses in the central nervous system. These pesticides are much less toxic to people, birds, and other vertebrates (animals with backbones) than earlier types of pesticides. So they seemed like a silver bullet—a breakthrough solution to a difficult problem. The EPA initially praised the pesticides as less risky than other types.

The first neonicotinoid was imidacloprid, which became available in the United States in 1994. Six other neonics soon followed. They were acetamiprid, clothianidin, nitenpyram, thiacloprid, thiamethoxam, and dinotefuran, the compound that killed the bees in the Oregon parking lot.

Since their introduction, neonics have become the most widely used pesticides in the world. Workers apply them in parks, on trees lining city streets, in residential yards, and on farms. Seed companies also spray neonics onto seeds before selling them to farmers. This coating gives seedlings a dose of pesticide as they start to grow. Seed companies claim that the pesticides ward off insect attacks before they occur. In 2011 farmers planted neonicotinoid-coated corn, cotton, and soybean seeds on roughly 104 million acres (42 million ha) just in the United States. That's an area about the size of California.

Although neonics may be safer for people and other vertebrates, they are highly toxic to beneficial insects, especially bees. Aimee Code of the Xerces Society calls them "silver bullets that misfired."

 ## LONG-LIVED AND MOBILE

All neonicotinoids share certain properties. They all stick around in plants and soil for months, sometimes years, after application. They all dissolve in water and can spread from one area to another through local waterways. Plants absorb them, and they spread throughout the entire plant, including to its pollen and nectar. When bees eat pesticide-contaminated pollen and nectar, they can become paralyzed and die.

It's clear from the bee kill in the parking lot in Wilsonville that high doses of neonics can kill bees. But even when neonics don't kill bees directly, they can still do harm. Laboratory studies show that bees exposed to extremely low doses of neonics can have trouble flying, navigating, and finding food. One study found that worker bumblebees exposed to neonics changed their behavior: they were less active and less likely to feed and care for the larvae. Other laboratory studies show that wild bees exposed to neonics produce fewer males and new queens, a change that could contribute to long-term population declines.

How much are these chemicals contributing to bumblebee declines? Finding answers to this question has proved to be difficult and controversial.

BAD NEWS FOR BEES

Although laboratory experiments show that even low doses of neonics can harm bees, especially bumblebees, the companies that make these chemicals have insisted that their products are safe for bees. Bayer Crop Science, a manufacturer of neonicotinoids, says, "The existing, extensive data consistently suggests that neonicotinoids, if used responsibly and in accordance with usage recommendations, do not represent an unacceptable risk to honeybees and other pollinators." Chemical companies charge that laboratory experiments that demonstrate the dangers of neonics don't represent "real world" exposures. They say scientists are giving bees bigger doses of neonics in the lab than bees would encounter outdoors.

Two studies published in the journal *Science* in 2017 reject the chemical company claims. These studies were done outdoors to test whether bees encounter harmful levels of neonics in real-life farm settings. One of the studies looked at three species of bees in three European countries (the United Kingdom, Hungary, and Germany). The study found that bumblebees exposed to neonics in farm fields produced fewer queens and that another type of wild bee laid fewer eggs. So neonics might not exterminate wild bees outright but might cause slow population declines over time.

The other study measured how much neonic pesticide honeybees were exposed to in cornfields in Canada. Then the researchers exposed honeybees to that same level of pesticide in an outdoor lab, far away from farm fields. The results? That amount of neonics affected honeybee health, reproduction, and survival. "I think it's reached a point now where no reasonable person would deny that these chemicals are impacting on bees one way or another," says Dave Goulson.

But are neonics contributing to the population declines of wild bees? Probably, although sorting out the role of neonics is messy.

TO BAN, OR NOT TO BAN?

A growing body of evidence suggests that neonicotinoids are bad for bees. In 2018 the European Parliament, an elected governing body of the twenty-eight member nations of the European Union, voted for an almost total ban on three widely used neonicotinoids. But in most parts of the world, neonics remain on the market.

In the United States, only a few restrictions were added. After the bee kill in Wilsonville, the Oregon Department of Agriculture banned the use of some neonicotinoids on linden trees. In 2016 during the administration of President Barack Obama, the US Fish and Wildlife Service phased out all uses of neonics in national wildlife refuges. This system of protected areas, set aside for conserving wildlife, encompasses about 150 million acres (61 million ha) in the United States. In announcing the ban, James Kurth, head of the National Wildlife Refuge System, wrote that neonic-treated seeds "can potentially affect a broad spectrum of non-target species" and would therefore be phased out.

In 2018 the administration of President Donald Trump reversed the ban. A memo from Fish and Wildlife Service deputy director Greg Sheehan said that instead of a ban, the use of neonics would be considered case by case. Farmers can apply to grow crops in some wildlife refuges. The memo stated that neonics might be necessary "to fulfill needed farming practices."

Environmental groups objected to the reopening of national wildlife refuge lands to neonicotinoids. "These are crucial wildlife sanctuaries, not to be sold to pad the bottom lines [profits] of pesticide companies," wrote George Kimbrell, legal director for the Center for Food Safety. Soon after the new policy announcement, the Center for Biological Diversity and the Center for Food Safety announced that they would sue the Trump administration, hoping to reverse the policy.

For one thing, exposure of bees to neonics in the wild varies widely. The concentration of neonics varies from plant to plant, and exposure varies from bee to bee.

And neonics could be interacting with other stressors on bees—stressors like *Nosema bombi*. Studies on neonicotinoids have shown that their toxicity to bees can worsen when used with a common fungicide, a chemical farmers spray to control fungal diseases on crops. How all these stressors interact is complicated and likely varies from species to species, and from place to place.

7

Bee Town, USA

Everything falls apart if you take pollinators out of the game.

—Dennis vanEngelsdorp, entomologist

To conserve bees, first, we have to know what they are, and whether they are in trouble. And that's a problem. With the exception of bumblebees, scientists are mostly in the dark about native bees.

As John Ascher put it, "We don't even know *what* native bees exist, as many remain undescribed or unidentifiable. Nor do we know *where* they live, as even state lists remain highly incomplete despite our best efforts. . . . As to *how* the bees are doing—we know even less."

We know even less about how native bees were doing fifty or one hundred years ago. Without the right historical data—for example, data showing just how abundant and diverse wild bees were in the past—it is difficult to draw conclusions about what is happening to wild bee populations in the present.

Charles Robertson studied bees in Carlinville, Illinois, at the turn of the last century. About one hundred years later, scientists Tiffany Knight and Laura A. Burkle studied Carlinville's bees again. This is one of the patches of forest where they collected bees.

Fortunately, the historical data exists in one place in America: Carlinville, Illinois.

From 1884 to 1916, Charles Robertson, a professor of biology and Greek at Blackburn College in Carlinville, drove around town in a horse and buggy, tramped into fields and woods, and documented which insects he saw on which flowers. He tallied fifteen thousand insect visits in all, and counted 214 bee species buzzing on 441 types of flowers.

Robertson was a pioneer. Not only did he collect the bees he saw, but in careful, handwritten records, he identified the species, wrote down which flowers they visited, and noted when the plants bloomed. He did this year after year for more than thirty years. His

Bee Town, USA

was one of the most intensive and careful studies of wild bees ever completed in one place.

His work gives us a rare look at the plant-pollinator networks that existed in the past. Because of his meticulous record keeping, modern scientists know exactly which bees were visiting which flowers in this one town more than one hundred years ago. That work gives modern scientists a rare opportunity: to revisit the town, tramp into its fields and woods, and see how its bees are holding up.

 ## ISLANDS FOR BEES

In the nineteenth century, the land around Carlinville was mostly prairie and forest. These sweeping natural landscapes, with a rich mix of native plants blooming throughout the seasons, met the habitat needs of bees.

But the landscape around Carlinville has changed. During the twentieth century, much of the prairie was converted to agriculture. By the 1970s, roughly 74 percent of the area was planted with crops or used as pasture for grazing animals. Forest cover had dwindled for the same reasons, although trees still stood along the streams. Similar changes in land use were taking place all across America. People plowed prairies, cut down forests, and turned large areas of land into farms, towns, and cities.

With the destruction of native landscapes, bees lost places to live. These changes affected both the common bees and the rare ones, both the generalists that forage on many different types of flowers and the specialists that depend on just one flower.

But people didn't destroy the native landscape wholesale. They left islands of habitat behind. Farmers left hedgerows along the edges of their fields to separate them. Towns and cities left patches of habitat in vacant lots, along streams, and on the edges of town. In these islands of habitat, spaced not too far apart, bees could continue to live.

REVISITING CARLINVILLE

The first scientists to follow up on Robertson's studies were Wallace E. LaBerge, an entomologist at the Illinois Department of Natural Resources, and John C. Marlin, who was then a college student and later became an entomologist. Between 1970 and 1972, they followed in Robertson's muddy footsteps and collected insects on some of the same plants in Robertson's studies. They published their work in the journal *Conservation Ecology*.

Had the passing of seventy-five years and significant changes to the landscape affected its diverse network of bees? Not much. Most of the bees from Robertson's time were still droning around in the early 1970s. The plant-pollinator networks—which bees visited which flowers—were remarkably similar to the ones Robertson had observed.

The two men attributed the resilience of bees to the islands of intact bee habitat: the hedgerows still standing between farm fields, the patches of woods still shading the stream banks. These islands of intact habitat ensured that Carlinville's bees continued to thrive.

SHRINKING ISLANDS

But the islands keep getting smaller. Since the late twentieth century, small family farms have been giving way to large, single-crop farms. On these farms, workers removed hedgerows and convert small, adjacent fields into giant fields planted with just one crop. Such big farms can produce more food at a lower cost than can small family farms. This economy of scale keeps food prices low. But big farms can be bad for bees.

Where bees once encountered a patchwork of crops and the occasional hedgerow, they now encounter acres and acres devoted to just a single crop, with no wildflowers in sight. This type of environment tends to be a bee desert.

At the same time, most cities and towns have sprawled outward

Industrial farms are bad for bees and other wildlife. The pesticides that farmers spray on crops can kill bees and pollute waterways. Industrial farms have also taken the place of meadows and woodlands where bees once made their homes.

with housing developments, business parks, and shopping centers. Bee habitat has been paved over or planted with lawns (dominated by a few species of wind-pollinated grasses), leaving bees without places to forage or nest. As agriculture and development has eaten up more land, less habitat remains for bees.

 ## BROKEN NETWORKS

In 2009 and 2010, another pair of researchers looked at Carlinville's famous bees. Ecologists Tiffany Knight and Laura A. Burkle retraced Robertson's studies, "trying to deduce what [Robertson] had done from old ledgers, specimen I.D. tags, and his privately published book *Flowers and Insects*," said Burkle.

"Robertson studied it all," added Knight. "He studied forests, he studied prairies, he studied roadside plants, he studied old fields; he even moved some plants to his own yard so he could study them more easily. If it was a species of flowering plant within a 10-mile [16 km] radius of Carlinville, it was in his study."

Knight and Burkle investigated which kinds of bees had visited which kinds of flowers in Robertson's time, as well as in LaBerge and Marlin's follow-up studies from the 1970s. They studied individual plant-pollinator pairings: one species of bee visiting one species of flower on a given day. If, on a different day, that same species of bee visited a flower of a different species that represented a second pairing. Taken together, the pairings added up to a complex plant-pollinator network.

To keep things simple in their study, Burkle and Knight looked at just one group of Robertson's plants: twenty-six wildflowers that bloom in early spring. They discovered that the passing of 120 years, and more changes to the landscape, had dramatically affected Carlinville's pollinators. In results published in 2013 in *Science*, they reported that the plant-pollinator networks had come unraveled.

On spring wildflowers, Robertson had documented 532 plant-pollinator pairings. But by 2010, 407 of those pairings—77 percent—had disappeared. The bees from Robertson's time were simply not visiting the same flowers. In fact, Burkle and Knight reported, *half* the bees associated with those pairings had disappeared. The researchers didn't see them anywhere.

 ## A BATH AND A BLOW-DRY

The pair of women also wondered whether, as the network came undone, bees were losing their effectiveness as pollinators. So they investigated one feature of plant-pollinator networks: how devoted a particular bee is to a particular flower. Some bees visit just one flowering species on a single day. That bee might spend an entire day flitting among the same type of flower, spreading pollen as it goes. This loyalty is good for pollination. It ensures that pollen from, for example, a sunflower spreads to other sunflowers.

Both Robertson, and later LaBerge and Marlin, had deposited the bees they collected in the Illinois Natural History Survey. These dead bees were still fuzzy with pollen. To assess whether bees were staying loyal to flowers, Knight and Burkle looked at the pollen dusting six species of bees, all captured while visiting a delicate pink flower known as spring beauty (*Claytonia virginica*). "We gave the [dead] bee a gentle bath and washed its pollen off onto a microscope slide," Knight said. "Then we fluffed [the bee] back up with a hair dryer."

They compared how much spring beauty pollen was on bees from the three different periods. If loyalty to flowers

Tiffany Knight and Laura A. Burkle studied *Claytonia virginica*, also known as spring beauty, to investigate plant-pollinator networks in Carlinville.

hadn't changed, their pollen load should look about the same. But the amount of spring beauty pollen on the bees that was high in Robertson's time, had declined in Marlin's study, and was even lower in 2010. It mixed with pollen from different kinds of flowers.

A bee carrying pollen from different flowers may not seem like a big deal, but it is an ominous sign. It indicates that bees could be losing their effectiveness as pollinators. If a bee coated with pollen from a flower visits a different kind of flower, pollination doesn't happen, because the bee is carrying the wrong type of pollen. If the wrong pollen falls from the bee's body onto the flower's female sex organ, the pollen doesn't do anything. The flower gets fertilized only if pollen from the same species of flower lands on the female sex organ. If Carlinville's bees are showing up on flowers coated with the wrong pollen, Carlinville's flowers will be less likely to make seeds and fruits. That could lead to fewer flowers to feed Carlinville's bees next year.

IT'S ALL IN THE TIMING

Finally, Knight and Burkle looked at one other way Carlinville was changing: a warming climate. Since Robertson's time, Earth's temperature has risen a little more than 1°F (0.6°C). Human activity, mainly the widespread burning of fossil fuels (petroleum, natural gas, and coal) brought on this warming. In the twentieth century, cars and trucks replaced the horse and buggy. On farms, petroleum-powered tractors replaced horses and mules. Coal-fueled factories spread across the United States and other industrialized nations. The burning of fossil fuels has pumped billions of tons of carbon dioxide into the air.

Carbon dioxide is a greenhouse gas. Unlike some atmospheric gases—such as nitrogen and oxygen—carbon dioxide traps heat from the sun and prevents it from escaping back into space. As industrialized nations have burned more and more fossil fuels, carbon dioxide has steadily accumulated in the air. The buildup of carbon dioxide is holding in more heat and causing Earth's climate to warm.

Burkle and Knight wondered how the warming climate was affecting Carlinville's bees. As the two women knew, a warming climate alters the timing of when flowering and other seasonal events occur. For bees and flowers, timing is everything. If spring warms up early, flowers can bloom early, and this can put bees out of sync with flowers.

Burkle and Knight were able to glimpse how this was playing

CRUSHED IN A CLIMATE VICE

One way climate change affects bees is by shifting where they can live. As the climate warms, and habitat that was once too cold becomes warmer, many species of plants and animals in the Northern Hemisphere are moving their ranges northward. For example, many birds are expanding their ranges northward.

But bumblebees aren't moving. In a study published in 2015 in *Science*, researchers analyzed roughly 423,000 sightings of sixty-seven different North American and European bumblebee species going back 110 years. They used the sightings to track where each of the species lived. They measured how far north or south each species lived, as well as the coldest and warmest temperatures it occupied.

They discovered that on both continents, bumblebees were retreating from the southern limits of their range by up to 190 miles (305 km). But the cold-weather bees weren't expanding northward into new places, perhaps because suitable habitat wasn't available to them. In the words of ecologist Jeremy Kerr of the University of Ottawa in Ontario, Canada, who led the study, "Climate change is crushing [bumblebee] species in a vice."

out because they had been careful in their choice of which flowers to study. They had chosen to look at early spring flowers. "If any community is going to be affected by climate change," Knight said, "it would be this one, because the plants flower soon after the winter snow melts."

The pair uncovered a mismatch between bees and flowers caused by climate change. Bees were crawling out of their winter hideaways eleven days earlier than they had in Robertson's time. Plants were flowering earlier too: an average of nine and a half days. At first glance, these changes might seem harmless. If bees and flowers are both early, they remain in sync. But Burkle and Knight found that the shifts caused problems for bees and flowers. Some bees emerged too early and were active before the right flowers were in bloom. And on average, flowers were blooming eight fewer days than in the past, and bees were flying twenty-one fewer days. That meant less time for pollination.

Burkle and Knight looked at their data and came to an important conclusion. Climate change was tugging on the already-frayed plant-pollinator networks, putting them under increased stress.

 ## THE LESSONS OF CARLINVILLE

Yet Carlinville offers a ray of hope. Burkle and Knight found that the old plant-pollinator networks had deteriorated over 120 years. But the researchers saw bees visiting flowers that they had not visited in Robertson's time. For example, eight bee species that had not visited the delicate pink spring beauty flowers visited them. The researchers observed a metallic greenish-gold species, *Lasioglossum cressonii*, visiting thirteen new flowers. It had visited none of these in Robertson's days. New connections were replacing broken ones.

This is one of the lessons of Carlinville: plant-pollinator networks are flexible. If one species of flowering plant dies off, often the pollinator that fed on that plant can find other flower species to pollinate. But the networks aren't infinitely flexible. At some point, the resilience of these networks may give way. Continuing climate change could put bees out of sync with their flowers, or bees could die off from disease or pesticides. The remaining bees may not be able to keep up with pollinating the flowers. "We can't just kick these plant-pollinator networks forever and expect them to keep functioning," Knight said.

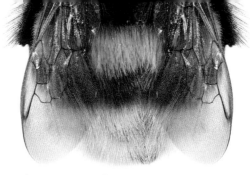

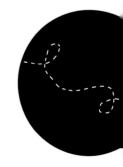

8

What's Best for Bees?

If plants . . . must have insects to exist, then human beings must have insects to exist. And not just one or two kinds of insects, such as the friendly and lovable honeybees, but lots of insect species, vast numbers of them.

—E. O. Wilson, biologist

Under a blue October sky, the gardens at Bald Eagle Area High School in Bellefonte, Pennsylvania, are abuzz with eight students in motion. Some pull weeds. Others push bulbs into the dirt or shovel compost the color of chocolate cake into a wheelbarrow. A young man named Kyle walks along a sidewalk, pruners in hand, looking for plants that have overgrown their bounds. At the center of the activity is teacher Todd Biddle, directing the students as they work.

Kyle points to a plant that is spilling into the walkway. "Mr. Biddle, should we cut this along the path?"

"Well, is it going over the walkway?" Biddle responds.

"Yeah, but not that much."

Another student calls out. "He's afraid if he cuts it, you're gonna cut his grade."

Bees pollinate the plants we rely on for food. So we need bees, and in the twenty-first century, bees need our help as well.

The rural school is converting islands of grass in the parking lot and narrow strips of grass along the brick building into habitat for pollinators. Purple asters are in bloom, attracting bees and butterflies, but many of the other flowers have faded, their stems and flower heads turning brown. "Most of these plants are only in bloom for a very short window," Biddle explains. That's okay, because the garden's purpose isn't to look perfect. "It's a garden that's here to feed insects."

"REDEFINE BEAUTIFUL"

Spurred into action by the decline of pollinators, people across the country are planting pollinator gardens in backyards, schoolyards,

What's Best for Bees?

parks, and neighborhoods. The purpose of these gardens is to feed the pollinators that feed us.

These gardens throw a lifeline to bees by giving them food and homes. All pollinator gardens have a few features in common. They all have flowers, preferably native flowers full of nectar and pollen. They have nesting sites, such as rodent holes or clumps of tall grass. They have places for bees to overwinter, such as patches of bare ground or rotting logs. They are free of synthetic pesticides that might harm bees.

Some people are helping beleaguered bees by changing how they mow their lawns. They create natural meadow by not mowing islands of their yard. Others are simply mowing less often. Mowing every two weeks is better for bees than weekly, because it allows bee-friendly weeds, such as clover and dandelion, to bloom.

Shaggy lawns. Rotting logs. Dead stems. Bare patches of dirt. Bee-friendly practices can look a little messy compared to a carpet of green grass. Pennsylvania master gardener Pam Ford, who teaches students and the public how to garden for pollinators, emphasizes that a garden should be more than merely pretty. It should be full of life. "We want to redefine beautiful."

 ## BOULEVARDS FOR BEES

If two neighbors each plant a pollinator garden with native plants, those gardens then form a corridor in which bees can travel. If corridors are near natural habitat corridors—such as along the edge of a field, along a stream, or on the edge of a forest—that forms an even larger corridor. These corridors can be almost anywhere: in cities and suburbs, on farms, and along roadways. Think of them as a boulevard for bees.

In Seattle, Washington, painter Sarah Bergmann is creating the Pollinator Pathway, a 1-mile (1.6 km) corridor that stretches between two green spaces: the Seattle University campus on one

Bees and butterflies land on flowers to collect nectar.

end and a patch of forest on the other. Bergmann and volunteers plant pollinator gardens along the pathway with the cooperation of homeowners, who agree to help maintain the gardens by pulling weeds and picking up litter.

Bergmann advocates that people think boldly about how to design the environment, especially in the era of climate change. She told National Public Radio: "I made the Pollinator Pathway to bring about a shift in environmental imagination. I'm saying that we aren't thinking big enough for the world we live in. It's about thinking less like conservationists, and a lot more like designers. Moving away from ideas of restoration and conservation, and moving toward the idea that we are active participants in the design of the planet."

 ## CITIZEN SCIENCE

To improve our understanding of wild bees, scientists say we need more people watching and monitoring them. To help with this effort, scientists have launched projects in which volunteers collect more data than researchers can gather on their own.

In the Great Sunflower Project, started by Gretchen LeBuhn,

What's Best for Bees?

an ecology professor at San Francisco State University, volunteers count bees across the United States and Canada. The goal is to gain a picture of where bees are doing well and where they're doing poorly. Volunteers don't have to be able to identify bee species— they simply have to be able to count. Typically, participants plant lemon queen sunflowers, a pollen-rich variety that is widely attractive to bees. Once the flowers bloom, each volunteer picks a warm morning and watches a flower for fifteen minutes, counting all the bees that visit. Some participants bring cameras and snap a photograph of each visiting bee. Volunteers then log their data online and upload any photos they have. By having thousands of people doing this, the project is helping to identify where bees are doing well and where they are struggling.

In 2014 the Xerces Society, in collaboration with several partners, launched Bumble Bee Watch. This citizen science project tracks the status of North American bumblebees. Participants across the United States and Canada snap photos of bumblebees and submit them online, along with the date, time, and location of the bee sightings. Volunteers use the website's identification guide to identify the species, and bumblebee experts verify the identity. Bumble Bee Watch has confirmed more than ninety-one hundred bumblebee sightings in the forty-nine states that have bumblebees (only Hawaii does not) and most Canadian provinces and territories.

FARMING FOR THE FUTURE

As awareness of the pollinator crisis grows, many people are calling for a system of agriculture that feeds people while also protecting the environment. This system is sustainable agriculture. It balances the demands of growing food with the need to conserve the environment for future generations. Sustainable agriculture recognizes that farms are an ecosystem, with interacting plants and animals.

HAWAII'S BEES

All Hawaiian bees are the descendants of a tiny, yellow-faced bee (*Hylaeus*) that somehow managed to reach the isolated Hawaiian Islands, located in the middle of the Pacific Ocean. That bee probably came from Japan or somewhere else in East Asia. But it's a mystery how the bee was able to cross about 4,000 miles (6,440 km) of open ocean. That original colonist evolved into sixty-three separate species—important pollinators of many of the islands' trees and shrubs.

In modern times, people have greatly changed the Hawaiian Islands. They have built towns and cities and cut down wilderness areas, destroying many native flowering plants. Without these plants to provide pollen, bees cannot survive. And humans have introduced many non-native plants to the islands. Some non-native plants have replaced plants that bees have long relied on for pollination. Non-native animals also harm bees. For example, in some places, feral (semi-wild) pigs have dug up the ground, changing the soil, resulting in grasslands where forests once grew.

With their habitat changed and destroyed, Hawaii's bees have struggled to survive. Most are in decline, many are very rare, and some may have gone extinct. In 2016 the United States gave endangered species status to seven of Hawaii's bee species. Yet it's not all bad news for Hawaii's bees. Eleven new species have been found since 2003.

"We can't put the genie back in the bottle [reverse the huge changes in agriculture], but we can integrate some of the best practices from the past into what we've learned about the future," says Claire Kremen, a conservation biologist at the University of California, Berkeley.

One sustainable approach is organic farming. Farmers who grow organic food emphasize the conservation of soil and water to protect the environment. They follow strict rules, including no synthetic pesticides. Some farmers release ladybugs or other natural predators into their fields to attack insect pests.

Another sustainable practice is integrated pest management. This scientific approach emphasizes that farmers first use nontoxic ways of treating pests—such as releasing insects such as ladybugs and wasps, which prey on insect pests—before resorting to chemical pesticides. When farmers use this approach, they dramatically lower their pesticide use—but do not eliminate it altogether.

A newer approach is integrated crop pollination. It involves a series of steps that farmers can take to promote wild pollinators on their farms. This approach encourages farmers to minimize pesticide risk to pollinators, using integrated pest management or organic methods, and to support diverse populations of wild bees. Some farmers are planting wildflower strips and hedgerows along their farms to feed wild pollinators and keep this winged workforce operating at peak efficiency.

Biologist Leithen M'Gonigle of Simon Fraser University in British Columbia, Canada, thinks the pollinator crisis could be "a kind of blessing in disguise" because "it forces us to think, 'What are we going to do to keep our food production going?' In the long term, it might be that we look back and say, 'Wow, this was a good thing, a good way of getting us to reprioritize and start thinking about conservation of native species.'"

HOW TO GET INVOLVED

Anyone can help conserve native bees. Here's how you can help:

- **Get to know bees.** Bees are fascinating to watch. The next time a bee buzzes by you, don't swat it. Follow it and observe. You might see it gathering nectar and pollen and flying off to its nest.

- **Become a citizen scientist.** Submit your sightings of bumblebees to Bumble Bee Watch (bumblebeewatch.org), or count bees in your garden for the Great Sunflower Project (greatsunflower.org). You can also look for bee monitoring programs in your area.
- **Buy organic, buy local.** Buy fruits and vegetables from local farmers who grow organically or use other bee-friendly farming practices (such as integrated pest management or integrated crop pollination).
- **Spread the word.** Many people are afraid of bees. Tell friends and family what you know about bees to help build more support for wild bees.

 ## PLANT A POLLINATOR GARDEN

You can also help native bees by growing a pollinator garden. It's okay to start small. All it takes is one native flowering plant. Over time, add more flowers to your garden. To attract the most bees, aim for native plants that bloom at different times of the year. Ultimately, your goal is to have flowers in bloom from early spring (willows and violets, for example) to late fall (goldenrods and sunflowers, for instance).

To attract ground-nesting bees, leave a small patch of bare soil in a sunny spot in your garden. As little as 1 square foot (0.09 sq. m) between clumps of flowers is enough. For bees that nest in twigs and other plant materials, plant perennials (plants that live for more than a year). Leave the dried stems of the plants on the ground through the winter. Or you can bundle a bunch of hollow stems of elderberry, bamboo, teasel, or yucca. If you cut just below the node (where new branches grow), one end should be naturally sealed. Align the stems (the open ends do not all need to point in the same direction), tie them together, and place the bundle in a sheltered spot out of the rain. Bees will overwinter in these spots.

You can help bees by growing a flower garden in your yard.

To keep bees healthy, don't use pesticides in your garden. When you buy plants for your garden, ask if the plants were treated with pesticides. If so, go elsewhere.

Besides creating a garden in your own yard, you can help create pollinator gardens in your community. Do a Google search to find pollinator gardens in local parks, at schools, and in your neighborhood.

✻   ✻   ✻

The decline of bees—across the country and around the world—is real. Some species of bumblebees are teetering on the brink of extinction and at least one, Franklin's bumblebee, may be gone forever. It is not any one thing that is killing bees. It's many things: diseases, pesticides, loss of habitat, and a changing climate.

But most wild bees can thrive if we help them. It's easy. Restore habitat for bees. Give them native flowers. Give them a place to nest. Protect them from pesticides. Grow food using bee-friendly practices. If enough of us do these things in enough places, even bees on the brink of extinction may come back.

What's Best for Bees?

A Note from the Author

About a decade ago, my children and I began to volunteer at the Snetsinger Butterfly Garden, a public pollinator garden in my Pennsylvania town. Working together, we sweated under the hot sun, pulling weeds and dead-heading flowers. I was initially drawn to the colorful butterflies that flitted past. But the Master Gardeners who ran the place talked mostly of bees—the many varieties, their importance, and their possible decline. Soon I too began to notice all the bees buzzing around—in the butterfly garden, around my town, and in my own backyard.

This book would not have been possible without the dedicated people who manage the pollinator garden, conduct scientific research there, and share their expertise and enthusiasm. In particular, I am indebted to the late Dr. Robert "Butterfly Bob" Snetsinger, who envisioned and built this amazing public garden. I also want to thank Pam Ford, who tirelessly promotes pollinator gardening and who has taught me that if you plant it, they will come.

I would like to thank a few other people who helped with this book: Todd Biddle and his students at Bald Eagle Area High School, Dr. Laura Burkle of Washington University, Dr. Jamie Strange of the US Department of Agriculture, and Justin Wheeler of the Xerces Society.

Lastly, I would like to thank my readers. The future rests in your hands. Build a patch of habitat. Protect it from pesticides. And the bees will come. I promise, they will come.

Glossary

angiosperm: any of a major group of plants that produce flowers, fruits, and seeds. Another name for angiosperms is flowering plants.

anther: the part of a flower that contains pollen and usually sits at the end of a stalk

climate change: the warming of Earth due to increased levels of carbon dioxide in the atmosphere, caused by the burning of fossil fuels

colony: a family unit of social bees, such as bumblebees, consisting of a queen, workers, and drones

conifer: a group of mostly evergreen trees and shrubs, usually having needle-shaped leaves and often having cones. Conifers include pines and firs.

deoxyribonucleic acid (DNA): a molecule found in the cells of all living things. DNA contains the instructions for how each organism will grow, function, and reproduce.

drone: a male bee whose job is to mate with a queen

ecologist: a biologist who studies the relationship between living things and their environment

ecosystem: a biological community of living things and their environment

endangered species: a species that is at serious risk of extinction

entomologist: a biologist who specializes in studying insects

evolution: the process by which organisms change over time, either randomly or in ways that enhance their chances of reproduction and survival. These changes can lead to the development of different species.

extinct: having no living members. A species becomes extinct when the last individual of the species dies.

fertilization: in plants, the fusion of pollen and egg to form a seed

forage: to travel around in search of wild food

fungus: a group of organisms that produce spores, including molds, yeast, and mushrooms. A few fungi can cause diseases.

habitat: the natural home of a living thing. A habitat is the place where an organism can find food, shelter, protection, and mates for reproduction.

invertebrate: an animal, such as an insect, that lacks a vertebrate, or backbone

native: living or growing naturally in a particular place

natural selection: the process, first proposed by naturalist Charles Darwin in 1859, by which organisms that are best adapted to their environment are more likely to survive and produce offspring

nectar: a sweet liquid produced by flowers

parasite: a living thing that lives with or on another thing, called the host. A parasite benefits from the relationship while harming the host in some way.

pathogen: a microbe such as a bacterium, fungus, or virus that causes disease

pesticide: a chemical substance used to kill harmful insects

pollen: tiny, dustlike particles produced in the anthers of a flower that fertilize the flower's eggs

pollination: the process of transferring pollen from the anther (male sex organ) to the stigma (female sex organ) of a flower

pollinator: an insect or other animal that transfers pollen within or between flowers, helping them make seeds

predator: an animal that lives by killing and eating other animals

queen: the fertile female of social bees whose purpose is to lay eggs

range: the region where a plant or animal naturally lives

species: a group of living things of the same type. Male and female members of the same species can breed (produce offspring) with one another.

worker: female bees that perform most of the work of the colony

Source Notes

6   Kathy Keatley Garvey, "Look Out, Franklin's Bumble Bee, They're Coming for You!," *Bug Squad* (blog), July 14, 2017, https://ucanr.edu/blogs/blogcore /postdetail.cfm?postnum=24673.

9   John D. Sutter, "The Old Man and the Bee," *CNN*, last modified December 13, 2015, https://www.cnn.com/2016/12/11/us/vanishing-sutter-franklins-bumblebee/ index.html.

10 Adam Federman, "Plight of the Bumblebee," *Earth Island Journal,* Autumn 2009, http://www.earthisland.org/journal/index.php/eij/article/plight_of_the _bumblebee/.

10 Federman.

12 Federman.

14 Rachel Carson, *Silent Spring* (New York: Houghton Mifflin Harcourt, 1962), 6.

19 Stephen Buchmann, *The Reason for Flowers: Their History, Culture, Biology, and How They Change Our Lives* (New York: Simon & Schuster, 2015), 31–32.

24 Sheila R. Colla, "The Truth about Bees," *Canadian Geographic*, May 17, 2018, https://canadiangeographic.ca/article/truth-about-bees.

25 Laura Tangley, "The Buzz on Native Pollinators," National Wildlife Federation, June 1, 2009, https://www.nwf.org/Magazines/National-Wildlife/2009/The-Buzz -on-Native-Pollinators.

28 Liz Langley, "Bumblebee Buzz Literally Makes Flowers Explode with Pollen," *National Geographic*, February 18, 2017, https://news.nationalgeographic .com/2017/02/honeybees-honey-insects-pollen-agriculture/.

30 Lisa C., "Mason Bees: Nature's Friendliest Pollinators," McLendon Hardware, February 10, 2016, https://www.mclendons.com/blog/post/mason-bees-natures -friendliest-pollinators.

31 Hillary Rosner, "Return of the Natives: How Wild Bees Will Save Our Agricultural System," *Scientific American*, September 1, 2013, https://www.scientificamerican .com/article/return-of-the-natives-how-wild-bees-will-save-our-agricultural-system/.

33 Dakin Henderson, "Wild Science: Bees and Climate Change," *High Country News*, September 2, 2015, https://truthout.org/video/wild-science-bees-and-climate -change/.

34 "A Ghost in the Making: Searching for the Rusty Patched Bumble Bee," Xerces Society for Invertebrate Conservation, accessed March 20, 2019, http://www .rustypatched.com/.

37 "Ghost in the Making."

37 Joseph O. Wilson and Olivia Messinger Carrill, *The Bees in Your Backyard: A Guide to North America's Bees* (Princeton, NJ: Princeton University Press, 2016), 9.

42 Goulson, *A Sting in the Tale: My Adventures with Bumblebees* (New York: Picador, 2013), 33.

43 Goulson, 33.

43 Goulson, 21.

48 John Muir, *My First Summer in the Sierra* (Boston: Houghton Mifflin, 1911), 110.

48 J. Weston Phippen, "Bumblebees Are Dying Out Because They're Too Fat to Mate," *Science*, February 7, 2017, https://www.theatlantic.com/science/archive /2017/02/rusty-patched-bumblebee-endangered-species/514388/.

50 Sutter, "Old Man and the Bee."

52 Goulson, *Sting in the Tale*, 170.

53 Goulson, 176.

56 "Ghost in the Making."

58 Jamie Strange, phone interview with author, July 26, 2018.

58 Strange.

59 Federman, "Plight of the Bumblebee."

61 Myrna E. Watanabe, "Colony Collapse Disorder: Many Suspects, No Smoking Gun," *Bioscience*, May 1, 2008, https://academic.oup.com/bioscience/article /58/5/384/234594.

62 E. O. Wilson, "My Wish: Build the Encyclopedia of Life," TED, March 2007, https:// www.ted.com/talks/e_o_wilson_on_saving_life_on_earth.

64 Ryan Gorman, "More Than 50,000 Bees Killed in Oregon, Insecticide Blamed in Largest Bee Die-Off in Recorded History," *Daily Mail* (London), June 23, 2013, http://www.dailymail.co.uk/news/article-2346864/More-50-000-bees-killed -Oregon-insecticide-blamed-largest-bee-die-recorded-history.html.

65 Carson, *Silent Spring*, 2–3.

66 Ker Than, "Organophosphates: A Common but Deadly Pesticide," *National Geographic*, July 18, 2013, https://news.nationalgeographic.com/news /2013/07/130718-organophosphates-pesticides-indian-food-poisoning/.

68 Aimee Code, "Neonicotinoids: Silver Bullets That Misfired," *Wings*, Fall 2015, http://www.gardenclub.org/resources/ngc-mpgc/Neonicotinoids-SilverBulletsThat Misfired_Wings-Fall2015.pdf.

69 Coralie van Breukelen-Groeneveld and Christian Maus, "The Bee Safety of Neonicotinoid Insecticides," Bayer Bee Care Center, October 2016, https:// beecare.bayer.com/bilder/upload/dynamicContentFull/Publications /BEEINFOrmed_issue3_The_Bee_Safety_of_Neonicotinoids-1iusc0izc.pdf.

69 Ashley P. Taylor, "Field Studies Confirm Neonicotinoids' Harm to Bees," *Scientist*, June 29, 2017, https://www.the-scientist.com/news-opinion/field-studies-confirm -neonicotinoids-harm-to-bees-31304.

70 James W. Kurth, "Use of Agricultural Practices in Wildlife Management in the National Refuge System," letter to regional refuge chiefs, July 17, 2014, available online at the Center for Food Safety, https://www.centerforfoodsafety.org/files /agricultural-practices-in-wildlife-management_20849.pdf.

70 Gregory J. Sheehan, "Withdrawal of Memorandum Titled, 'Use of Agricultural Practices in Wildlife Management in the National Refuge System (July 17, 2014),'" letter to service directorate, available online at Center for Biological Diversity, https://www.biologicaldiversity.org/campaigns/pesticides_reduction/pdfs/2018 -8-2-FWS-memo-GMO-Neonics-on-wildlife-refuges.pdf.

70 Austin Price, "Trump's Interior Department Reverses Ban of Pesticides in Wildlife Refuges," *Sierra*, August 9, 2018, https://www.sierraclub.org/sierra/trump-s -interior-department-reverses-ban-pesticides-wildlife-refuges.

72 Seth Borenstein, "UN Science Report Warns of Fewer Bees, Other Pollinators," AP, February 26, 2016, https://apnews.com/b1d7229217ac45b6a1681b8cdcbabe90.

72 Sarah Fecht, "Hive and Seek: Domestic Honeybees Keep Disappearing, but Are Their Wild Cousins in Trouble, Too?," *Scientific American*, May 8, 2012, https:// www.scientificamerican.com/article/hive-and-seek-domestic-honeybees-keep -disappearing/.

76 Diana Lutz, "Walking in the Footsteps of 19th- and 20th-Century Naturalists, Scientists Find Battered Plant-Pollinator Network," Washington University, February 28, 2013, https://source.wustl.edu/2013/02/walking-in-the-footsteps-of -19th-and-20thcentury-naturalists-scientists-find-battered-plantpollinator-network/.

76 Lutz.

78 Lutz.

80 Cally Carswell, "Bumble Bees Being Crushed by Climate Change," *Science*, July 9, 2015, https://www.sciencemag.org/news/2015/07/bumble-bees-being-crushed -climate-change.

80 Lutz, "Walking."

81 Lutz.

82 Stephen L. Buchmann and Gary Paul Nabhan, *The Forgotten Pollinators* (Washington, DC: Island, 1997), xiv.

82 Conversation heard by author at Bald Eagle Area High School, Bellefonte, Pennsylvania, 2018.

83 Todd Biddle, interview with author, May 27, 2018.

84 Pam Ford, interview with author, August 18, 2016.

85 Adam Frank, "Why Honeybees Are the Wrong Problem to Solve," *National Public Radio*, June 13, 2017, https://www.npr.org/sections/13.7/2017/06/13/532729268 /why-honeybees-are-the-wrong-problem-to-solve.

87 Sarah Schmidt, "Beauty and the Bees," Xerces Society, July 2010, https://xerces .org/2010/07/21/beauty-and-the-bees/.

88 Rosner, "Return of the Natives."

Selected Bibliography

Buchmann, Stephen. *The Reason for Flowers: Their History, Culture, Biology, and How They Change Our Lives*. New York: Simon & Schuster, 2015.

Burkle, Laura A., John C. Marlin, and Tiffany M. Knight. "Plant-Pollinator Interactions over 120 Years: Loss of Species, Co-Occurrence, and Function." *Science* 29 (2013): 1611–1615.

Cameron, Sydney A., Haw Chuan Lim, Jeffrey D. Lozier, Michelle A. Duennes, and Robbin Thorp. "Test of the Invasive Pathogen Hypothesis of Bumble Bee Decline in North America." *Proceedings of the National Academy of Sciences* 113, no. 6 (2016): 4386–4391.

Carson, Rachel. *Silent Spring*. New York: Houghton Mifflin, 1962.

Code, Aimee. "Neonicotinoids: Silver Bullets That Misfired." *Wings*, Fall 2015, 16–21.

Embry, Paige. *Our Native Bees: North America's Endangered Pollinators and the Fight to Save Them*. Portland, OR: Timber, 2018.

Federman, Adam. "Plight of the Bumblebee." *Earth Island Journal*, Autumn 2009. http://www.earthisland.org/journal/index.php/eij/article/plight_of_the_bumblebee/.

Garvey, Kathy Keatley. "Robbin Thorp's Mission: Saving Franklin's Bumble Bee." UC Davis Department of Entomology and Nematology, July 27, 2010. http://entomology.ucdavis.edu/News/Robbin_Thorps_Mission__Saving_Franklins_Bumble_Bee/.

Goulson, Dave. *A Sting in the Tale: My Adventures with Bumblebees*. New York: Picador, 2013.

Marlin, John C., and Wallace E. LaBerge. "The Native Bee Fauna of Carlinville, Illinois, Revisited after 75 Years: A Case for Persistence." *Conservation Ecology* 5, no. 1 (June 2001): 9.

Moisset, Beatriz, and Stephen Buchmann. *Bee Basics: An Introduction to Our Native Bees*. Washington, DC: USDA Forest Service, 2011.

Phippen, J. Weston. "Bumblebees Are Dying Out Because They're Too Fat to Mate." *Atlantic*, February 7, 2017. https://www.theatlantic.com/science/archive/2017/02/rusty-patched-bumblebee-endangered-species/514388/.

Rosner, Hillary. "Return of the Natives: How Wild Bees Will Save Our Agricultural System." *Scientific American*, September 1, 2013. https://www.scientificamerican.com/article/return-of-the-natives-how-wild-bees-will-save-our-agricultural-system/.

Sutter, John D. "The Old Man and the Bee." *CNN*. Last modified December 13, 2016. https://www.cnn.com/2016/12/11/us/vanishing-sutter-franklins-bumblebee/index.html.

Wilson-Rich, Noah. *The Bee: A Natural History*. Princeton, NJ: Princeton University Press, 2014.

Further Information

Books

Blevins, Wiley. *Ninja Plants: Survival and Adaptation in the Plant World*. Minneapolis: Twenty-First Century Books, 2017. Plants use all sorts of tricks to attract pollinators, spread their seeds, repel predators, and secure food for themselves. Wiley Blevins introduces some of the "ninja" practices.

Holm, Heather. *Bees: An Identification and Native Plant Forage Guide*. Minnetonka, MN: Pollination, 2017. This book includes detailed information about native bees in the central and eastern United States and Canada and gives guidance on what trees, shrubs, and flowers to plant for bees in these locations.

Hughes, Meredith Sayles. *Plants vs. Meats: The Health, History, and Ethics of What We Eat*. Minneapolis: Twenty-First Century Books, 2016. What is the best diet? That's a personal decision, but some modern food-growing practices endanger pollinators and other wildlife. This book explores cultural, ethical, and environmental reasons for choosing certain foods.

Milhaly, Christy, and Sue Heavenrich. *Diet for a Changing Planet: Food for Thought*. Minneapolis: Twenty-First Century Books, 2018. As Earth's human population grows and as climate change disrupts traditional food systems, how can we feed everyone? One solution: eat insects! This book explores this and other unconventional food sources.

Williams, Paul, Robbin Thorp, Leif Richardson, and Sheila Colla. *Bumblebees of North America: An Identification Guide*. Princeton, NJ: Princeton University Press, 2014. Are you ready to get out into the field and start identifying bumblebees? This guide tells you how to identify all forty-six species of North American bumblebees north of Mexico.

Wilson, Edward O. *The Diversity of Life*. New York: W. W. Norton, 1992. The author reflects on evolution, how the living world became diverse, and how people are destroying that diversity.

Wilson, Joseph S., and Olivia J. Messinger Carrill. *The Bees in Your Backyard: A Guide to North America's Bees*. Princeton, NJ: Princeton University Press, 2016. The authors offer an entertaining introduction to native bees of the mainland United States and Canada.

Websites and Online Videos

Bumble Bee Watch
http://www.bumblebeewatch.org
This citizen science project collects bumblebee observations in North America.

A Ghost in the Making: Searching for the Rusty Patched Bumble Bee
http://www.rustypatched.com/
This documentary film follows a nature photographer's quest to find the once-common, now rare, rusty patched bumblebee.

The Great Sunflower Project
https://www.greatsunflower.org
This citizen science project counts and identifies bees visiting flowers.

"Raising Bumble Bees at Home: A Guide to Getting Started"
https://www.ars.usda.gov/ARSUserFiles/20800500/BumbleBeeRearingGuide.pdf
Do you want to try raising bumblebees at home? Start with this step-by-step guide from the US Department of Agriculture.

USGS Native Bee Laboratory—Instagram
https://www.instagram.com/usgsbiml/
Check out gorgeous pictures of native bees from the team at the USGS Native Bee Inventory and Monitoring Lab.

Wild Science: Bees and Climate Change
https://www.hcn.org/articles/wild-science-video-colorado-bees-flowers-and-climate-change/
This short film from High Country News focuses on the research of Rebecca Irwin, an ecologist at North Carolina State University. She studies how climate change is affecting bees.

Xerces Society for Invertebrate Conservation
http://www.xerces.org/bumblebees
Learn more about the biology and conservation of bumblebees and other pollinators, and find helpful tips on how to grow a pollinator garden with lists of native plants by region.

Index

agriculture
  industrial-scale, 32,
    50–51, 59, 75–76
  and pesticides, 32, 59,
    61, 64, 67–71, 76,
    81, 88
  and pollination, 33
  sustainable, 86–88
angiosperms, 18, 21, 23
  See also flowering
  plants

bee colonies, 29, 32,
    40–47, 52, 58,
    60–61, 63
bees. *See*
    also bumblebees;
    honeybees
  anatomy of, 34–36
  and climate change,
    79–81, 85, 91
  evolution of, 18–21,
    27, 87
  foraging by, 13, 16, 30,
    32, 42–43, 45–46,
    53, 55, 74, 76
  habitat of, 10, 12–13,
    41, 74–76, 80,
    83–84, 87, 91
  nesting of, 29, 36,
    40–47, 76, 84, 89,
    91
  ranges of, 8, 10, 12,
    59, 80
  reproduction of, 42–43,
    46–47, 58, 69
beestings, 36, 44

bumblebees
  colonies, 40–43,
    45–47, 52, 58, 63
  commercial, 50–56,
    58–59
  life cycle of, 42–44
Bumble Bee Watch, 86,
    89
buzz pollination, 27, 30,
    41

Carlinville, IL, 73–81
Carson, Rachel, 14,
    65–67
climate change, 79–81,
    85, 91
colony collapse disorder
    (CCD), 60–61
corbiculae, 21, 35
Cretaceous period,
    14–15, 19–21
cuckoo bees, 36, 38

Darwin, Charles, 19
deoxyribonucleic acid
    (DNA), 20, 56
dichloro-diphenyl-
    trichloroethane
    (DDT), 66–67
drones, 40, 42–47, 58, 68

Endangered Species Act,
    8–10, 12
evolution
  of bees, 18–21, 27, 87
  of flowering plants,
    18–21
extinction, 8–11, 22, 31,
    87, 91

flies, 16, 18, 26, 31, 37
flowering plants, 76
  evolution of, 18–21
  reproduction of, 16–21
Franklin's bumblebee,
    6–11, 50, 54–55, 91

Great Sunflower Project,
    85–86, 89

honey, 32, 46–47
  storing of, 32
honeybees
  colonies, 29, 32, 40,
    44–47, 60–61
  commercial, 28–30,
    32, 60–61
  life cycle of, 46–47

nectar
  bees foraging for, 7,
    16, 22, 25, 42, 46,
    85, 88
  in bee diet, 41, 59, 61,
    68, 84
  in making honey, 32,
    45
  non-bees drinking, 26
  pesticides and, 68
  use of proboscis to
    drink, 21, 28, 35
neonicotinoids, 64, 67–71
Nosema bombi, 54–59,
    71

organophosphates,
    66–67

pesticides, 32, 50, 57, 59,
  61, 63–71
plant reproduction,
  15–21, 41
pollination
  carried out by bees,
    15, 18, 23, 27–28,
    41–43, 47
  carried out by
    non-bees, 16, 18–23
  commercial, 29–30,
    32, 50–61
  of food plants, 28–31
  by humans, 32–33

pollinator gardens,
  82–85, 89–90
Pollinator Pathway,
  84–85

queen bees, 40–47, 54,
  58, 60, 68–69

Robertson, Charles,
  73–81
rusty patched bumblebee,
  11–13, 49

scopa, 21, 35

waggle dance, 47
wasps, 9, 14, 18, 20–21,
  37–38, 88
worker bees, 40, 43–47,
  50, 60, 68

Photo Acknowledgments

Image credits: Design: Kletr/Shutterstock.com; Content: Rike/iStockphoto/Getty Images, p. 7; Linda Rosier/NY Daily News Archive//Getty Images, p. 11; © Clay Bolt/Minden Pictures, p. 12; FollowScience Photo Library - LEONELLO CALVETTI/Getty Images, p. 15; Laura Westlund/Independent Picture Service, pp. 17, 36, 46; Spencer Arnold Collection/Hulton Archive/Getty Images, p. 19; Kutub Uddin/500px Prime/Getty Images, p. 22; JLGutierrez/Getty Images, p. 25; ShaunWilkinson/iStockphoto/Getty Images, p. 26; Jamie Hooper/Alamy Stock Photo, p. 29; Betty Shelton/Shutterstock.com, p. 30; Michael Willis/Alamy Stock Photo, p. 33; ElementalImaging/Getty Images, p. 35; Sam Droege/USGS Bee Inventory and Monitoring, p. 39; Thomas Koschnick/Alamy Stock Photo, p. 40; Mim Friday/Alamy Stock Photo, p. 41; nayneung1/iStockphoto/Getty Images, p. 45; MAURO FERMARIELLO/SCIENCE PHOTO LIBRARY/Getty Images, p. 49; Hendrik Schmidt/picture alliance//Getty Images, p. 51; Soumendra Chowdhury/500px//Getty Images, p. 55; AP Photo/Jimmy May, p. 60; RAYMOND ROIG/AFP/Getty Images, p. 63; Costas Metaxakis/AFP/Getty Images, p. 65; Alfred Eisenstaedt/The LIFE Picture Collection/Getty Images, p. 66; Courtesy Laura Burke, p. 73; fotokostic/iStockphoto/Getty Images, p. 76; Gail Jankus/Science Source/Getty Images, p. 78; markhortonphotography/Getty Images, p. 83; Kuttelvaserova Stuchelova/Shutterstock.com, p. 85.

Cover: Kletr/Shutterstock.com.

About the Author

Rebecca E. Hirsch holds a PhD in cellular and molecular biology from the University of Wisconsin. She enjoys writing about science and discovery for children and young adults. Her books for young readers include *The Human Microbiome: The Germs That Keep You Healthy* and *De-Extinction: The Science of Bringing Lost Species Back to Life*. A trained plant biologist and lifelong gardener, she grows native plants and watches bees in her own backyard. She lives with her family in State College, Pennsylvania. Learn more at rebeccahirsch.com.